GREEN THOUGHTS AND MEMORIES

Marina Schinz

Scheidegger & Spiess

For Larry, again...

When my first book on gardens, *Visions of Paradise*, came out and proved to be a success, my publisher, Andrew Stewart, eagerly asked how long it would take me to come up with a second volume. Half-jokingly I replied, "Twenty years." Decades have raced by and it is now even longer than that. During that interval, my husband Lawrence Rubin and I led busy lives. We moved several times, first from New York City to Katonah, which is at the northern periphery of Westchester, and then further upstate to Dutchess County in New York, where we built a house, tended the landscape, and made a garden from scratch. The farmed fields surrounding our property became part of our existence as we followed with curiosity what our neighbors were up to, which led to our enthusiastically joining the Dutchess Land Conservancy organization that had recently been formed. Its scope was to limit invasive developments and map out where new buildings should be allowed so as not to hamper the farmers' work or interfere with the scenery. It stood out as an institution for its enlightened attitude, the beauty of the landscape being high up its agenda: America at its best.

In 1995 we left the States and moved to Europe, where we acquired an abandoned villa in northern Italy, which we restored and to which we added orchards and a vineyard. Here too the rural atmosphere with its aura of time-honored traditions sets the scene. As an ongoing project it substantially increased my knowledge of horticulture and gave me the perspective from which this book is written. We also travelled extensively, visiting many verdant habitats wherever we went. And now that I find myself, seemingly overnight, at the threshold of maturity, I have become conscious that our relationship to nature changes and varies from one person to the next, much like our handwriting or our fingerprints. This notion of individual sensibility gave me the idea to trace the green line that meanders through my life. Maybe it will be distinguishable from someone else's. Or it may show how many of us pass through similar stages, from childhood to dotage, from sandbox to tombstone, the seven ages of women and of men.

But neither am I Thoreau writing in the wilderness in that sonorous voice and well-forged prose, nor could I be compared to a foxhunting English country lady, practiced in all aspects of husbandry and steeped in horticulture. I am simply someone who loves the company of plants. I also have a great appetite for looking at images of every kind. That I see the world as through a frame makes me wonder if a good fairy placed a viewfinder in my cradle so that I would become a photographer. For that is the trade I plied. At a serendipitous moment in my younger days my craft espoused the pictorial side of horticulture and I had the luck to make myself a name in that field. For my own edification I embarked on a study of the different themes and variations in the garden, which found its way into print as the aforementioned book. By sheer contagion I became a gardener myself, facing the triumphant successes and the heartbreaking disappointments that come with that terrain. Many green thoughts crossed my mind, and whenever an image presented itself to highlight the elements that go into the making of a garden my camera was at hand. From my vast archive of photographs taken over the past fifty years I selected my favorite ones to include in this book.

Although I gardened in different climates, I am not an expert. My approach is of the broad-brush, slapdash, trial-and-error kind. The failures we gardeners face are numerous, and what sometimes seems to grow best is the assessment of our ineptitude. Even Vita Sackville-West, the dashing gardener, writer, and owner of Sissinghurst Castle, did not always get her way. She had a box she called the morgue, in which she kept the labels of her departed plants. I do not have a box, but a deep hole for the hapless individuals I discard, giving them a chance to decompose and remain an integral part of my garden in the form of loam.

Once I became a seasoned insider my viewpoint shifted from the pictorial toward the empirical. The defining role of the climate, the chemistry of the soil, and the plan and construction of a garden revealed themselves to be of capital importance. Labor, on account of its reduced availability, also has to be reckoned with. The plants we fancy must be seen in the light of their affordability, and I am not talking about the price of purchase, but how much water they guzzle and what kind of maintenance they require. I observe flowers, grass, shrubs, and weeds in an ever-changing light as they move in and out of my reach, sometimes forcing me into a new direction.

As most people know, gardens, unlike paintings or embroideries, are never finished. They are ephemeral creations suspended between past and future. Typically, when cultivating our potager or flowerbed we are caught up in fantasies of what it will look like next year, never mind what a mess we are currently faced with. Pure optimism keeps us happily digging, clipping, and replanting since a sense of an already outlined rosy future propels us forward. Tomorrow is another day, says Scarlett O'Hara, squeezing a clump of soil in her hand. I hope hers was less clayish than mine.

White Strawberries

Some gardens are forever finalized. I am not talking about cemeteries, but about the places we store in our memory. Filtered through the fine mesh of our recollection, they have acquired a texture of their own, like a rare old Burgundy that over many years has become ennobled by a depth and roundness you don't get in a Beaujolais Nouveau. I had the good fortune of growing up in a large garden in Switzerland and traveling from time to time to my grandmother's domaine in Naples, far away from home. Neither of these gardens exist anymore, but they left their imprint and reside in an indelible part of my mind. It is to them that I owe my desire for space, a sense of harmony, and a strong inclination to busy myself outdoors.

My childhood home was a Roman villa my grandfather had built 1,000 kilometers from its source of inspiration, on a hill above Zurich, overlooking that old and prosperous Swiss city. Loftily situated just below the crest of a southwest-facing slope, it was simply known as "the villa" and fully deserved this name, for it was modeled after the dwellings that Arnoldo Ruesch, my mother's father, had admired in Pompeii in his youth. He was born and grew up in Naples as the son of a Swiss family that was among the numerous foreigners to settle in Naples during the 1860s. The new government encouraged entrepreneurs from other countries to set up their businesses and industries in that young nation, Italy. Upon their arrival, the Rueschs had acquired a printing establishment by the name of Richter & Co. which they, with Swiss zeal and efficiency, were able to turn into a blossoming modern enterprise. As a leading printing press and design firm, "la Richter" had secured itself the right to print tourist posters for the Italian railway, official government forms, and—best of all—bank notes for the Banco di Napoli, which were legal tender in Italy. Truth be told, the young Arnoldo—he was the middle of three sons—had little interest in the printing business except for withdrawing funds to pursue his passion for archeology. He had become an enthusiastic collector of Roman antiquities and, since excavations in Pompeii and Herculaneum were continuously taking place, was able to put together a remarkable collection of Roman objects, fresh from the grave and warm from the press, so to speak. Once he had had his fill of Naples, he started to look around for a spot where he could build himself a home and private museum to house his treasures, preferably at a safe distance from Naples and far from his wife, who had sworn she would never live further north than Rome. He found what he was looking for in 1910, north of the Alps in the country of his ancestors, and started a new life in Zurich, leaving his wife and two children behind.

In my opinion, Zurich's turf was not a perfect location for Arnoldo Ruesch to build his dream house on, because the Pompeiian dwellings of 2,000 years ago were conceived for maximum ventilation in a hot climate and not for the rains

Villa Rüesch in Zurich

Peristyle

Atrium

Inner courtyard

and winters of Switzerland. His one-story villa was a faithful reproduction of a Pompeiian summer residence, complete with atrium and peristyle, richly decorated with built-in original mosaics and frescoes. It had an open inner courtyard with an impluvium at its heart: that rectangle around which the whole house is conceived. This central little garden was shady and cool, causing endless draughts in the house. It came into its own only during the few dog days of summer, which I felt occurred all too rarely. The snow in winter, on the other hand, settled down nicely and took forever to melt, while my parents, way ahead of their time, groaned about the heating bills decades before oil prices hit the ceiling.

Alas, the social climate of this sober Zwinglian city revealed itself as similarly inclement. Unhelpful rumors arose in town about the orgiastic goings-on in the villa on the hill, where Arnoldo staged parties at his posh Pompeiian pad, where his guests were purportedly gallivanting around clad in bedsheets and adorned with Roman jewelry borrowed from the collection of their host. This kind of hedonism did not go down well with the virtuous burghers of Zurich, so before long Arnoldo moved on to the greener pastures of Paris, where he became infatuated with a Jewish lady by the name of Mademoiselle Fuchs. He married her on his early deathbed. Luckily for us she renounced any claim to his property in Switzerland. Upon his death, my mother, half Italian and half Swiss, took over the Zurich property; she was only nineteen at the time and continued to live in that most unusual mansion to the end of her days. And that is how I came to grow up in a Roman villa, in a place I probably would not have chosen on my own.

The garden surrounding our villa was more in keeping with the local spirit than the house and its contents. Either my grandfather had fewer eccentric notions or he fell on a sound advisor regarding the outdoors. Our property was larger and simpler than what I saw in our neighborhood. The center of our summer life was a terrace on the main facade of the house, from where we had a magnificent view of the city and the shimmering lake below. The terrace wall and its railings were covered in clematis and ivy. Two Corinthian capitals—the real thing—punctuated its ends, from where a staircase descended on each side, leading to two symmetric platforms, each shaded by a horse chestnut. A few more steps connected this area near the house to a large lawn that rolled softly toward the lower end of our land, a good stretch further down, where an evergreen hedge camouflaged an iron fence and screened us from the street. A certain simplicity set the tone of our place, which impressed the visitor more by its prestigious site and by the generosity of its space than by elaborate plantings.

Like the typical *Herrschaftsgarten* built around the turn of the century, it had a number of features that were considered de rigueur. Upon entering through an imposing iron gate, a graveled driveway flanked by shrubs led uphill and then wound around to a spacious entrance court, formed by the columned north facade of the villa and a semicircular retaining wall on the opposite side. An authentic Roman sarcophagus turned into a fountain graced that wall and served as an eyecatcher when one stepped out of the large main door. Various amphoras and sculptures, also the real thing, were scattered around here and there. To complete the Mediterranean illusion, two wooden tubs with oleanders, progressively less lush after each inhospitable winter, were removed from their temporary shelter and put out in spring. Whatever was movable was carefully stored away in the fall, including the tons of gravel that covered the driveway and the entrance court, lest some of it should be irretrievably lost when the snow plow was put to work, occasionally wreaking havoc.

Along the east side of the square house ran a flower bed containing the usual boring sequence of municipal bedding plants. The pansies mixed with the forget-me-nots and the red and yellow tulips of springtime were replaced with red salvias, powder-blue ageratum, and begonias in early summer. It was only much later during my travels to England that I became acquainted with the full potential of foundation borders, where small shrubs and perennial flowers can soften the silhouette of rigid architecture and enrich them with botanical delights. The only Anglo-Saxon feature we had was a small rectangular croquet lawn, parallel to the east side of the house—the beckoning view from our bedrooms. It was full of tiny flowering weeds, and we played exhilarating matches there from croquet to badminton, pétanque, and whatever the game of the day was. I also took my first advertising picture on that lawn when I was twelve, having Ovomaltine in mind as a client. I did it on spec. (It is, by the way, still available.)

The maintenance of the garden proper was entrusted to a full-time gardener, who doubled as a chauffeur and lived in the cottage on the second floor above the garage. What occupied most of his working hours was the intensely cultivated expanse of vegetable plots and rows of cutting flowers, along with all the appurtenances that a well-kept kitchen garden requires. There was a greenhouse to start seedlings in and cold frames to harden them off, trellises for training blackberries, and a special support for sweet peas, those lovely, intensely fragrant flowers that are grown in the kitchen garden since they are meant for picking. And of course there was an area in the shade for compost in the making and next to it a huge pile of fluffy humus: the sow's ear having been turned into a silk purse. Everything was there, very neatly kept. The only uneven patches were the disagreements my mother had with the gardener about which vegetables to grow and when to pick them. Fewer cabbages please, and not that many kohlrabi either. It was important to her that finer vegetables be harvested when small; peas especially had to be gathered at a very early stage. The few times she won a round in this ongoing battle, these tiny peas were served at our table Italian-style in a soup terrine and eaten as a first course with a spoon. This delicacy no longer exists, as the taste has been bred out of "English" peas and other vegetables in pursuit of lesser features such as disease resistance and size. To many an exacting gourmet this is a real tragedy, and in the tomato world one of deplorable dimension. Seeing the sign F1 on a label has the same effect on me as the word "enriched" on a bag of flour. It's a step too far in the wrong direction. So as not to come across as a total pessimist I would like to mention that we now also can grow many fruits and vegetables that have been im-proved. Raspberries, for instance, are nothing short of fabulous today, especially since their season has been extended well into the cooler months. Early, middle, and late fruiting raspberry varieties are a better choice than repeated fruiting ones, but that is a matter of personal preference. I'd rather have the big bang than a series of little squirts.

Among the highlights in our garden were the extensive strawberries beds. When a bumper crop was in sight, my school buddies were invited over for picking and eating. I ran into one of them not long ago and he still remembered all the fun and mischief we had in the berry patch. No pleasure compares to eating ripe fruit direct-ly from the plant—a good reason for not spraying. When I was nine years old my father allotted me a patch of my own, to do with as I pleased. Since I was too busy in those days to tend the 1 x 2-meter bed, I ran to the gardener and begged him to plant my entire plot with *fraises des bois*. Armchair gardening seems to have been an innate instinct at the time and I regularly visited my little strawberry field to check on its progress. Even today I consider alpine strawberries the hands-down winners for beauty of plant, blossom, and fruit, as well as procurers of the purest taste and enticing fragrance, still producing blossoms when the first berries mature. They are quite easy to look after, as long as it is a variety that does not make runners. But the real epiphany in this, my first little garden, was the moment when I discovered a plant that had albino strawberries. They were plump and perfectly shaped and pure white without a trace of color. I closed my eyes to taste one. The burst of flavor was as intense as that of the red ones and I was tickled pink. It was my first whiff of a horticultural rarity, and I kept visiting that particular specimen every few days to make sure that the fruits had not suddenly reverted to red. This seminal event turned on the switch of my botanical curiosity, which lasted through my whole life. I did not encounter white strawberries again for decades until I was invited to dinner at Rosemary Verey's lovely country house at Barnsley, where a bowl of mixed berries was served for dessert. Rosemary was one of the most accomplished gardeners of her generation, and her berries looked like veritable jewels in the large bowl. The mound of black, red, and blue berries was studded with little white *fraises des bois* as if with diamonds. It confirmed my opinion of Rosemary as one of the great gardeners of the twentieth century. Which she actually was, even without the white strawberries.

My father's pet plant in the garden, on the other hand, had only academic and no gustatory interest, and it too required frequent inspection. It was a seedling of a dawn redwood which before 1941 was only known from fossils, and was believed at the time to be a very rare specimen. When it keeled over we had to bemoan its death as a dramatic event of historic proportion. Given its scrawny aspect I can't say that I was deeply grieved, since I definitely am a sucker for good looks.

The real splendor of our property, however, was our extensive native woods, fenced in and secure, full of healthy beeches, conifers, hazels, oaks, ash trees, and many others, without a lot of undergrowth, allowing white anemones and yellow cowslips to make their unhampered appearance in early April. Though they belonged to us, these woods had to be maintained under the close supervision of the city's forestry department. No tree could be touched without the permission of the *Stadtförster*, the official overseer who dropped by every year to designate which trees could or should be cut down. My father accompanied him on his rounds and usually tried to convince him to take down a tree or two at the edge of the wood, hoping to pry away a couple of meters from the green zone and make the land more valuable, which of course never worked because the Swiss are sticklers for correct recordkeeping. When you drive through their picture-perfect countryside you can see how richly such excellent administration pays off.

Once I had gotten ahold of the names of the horse chestnuts, maples, oaks, walnuts, larches, firs, and beeches that surrounded me, I began to wonder how I could ever have lived without knowing them. Some of these large trees were our favorite companions and the center of many games and activities. For years we climbed around in them playing Robin Hood, with bows made from hazel wood and string. Later we suspended rope ladders and a trapeze on sturdy branches to indulge our fantasy in our future career as circus artists. Exciting treasure hunts and "archeological" digs brought us deeper into the woods to increase the mystery of these adventures. What I did not care for, however, were our summer hikes in the Swiss Alps above the altitude of 2,400 meters, where trees cannot grow and where a strange desolation settled over my soul. I simply don't want to live without trees.

It is in these woods and meadows that my earliest childhood played itself out, leaving no doubt that this was what the rest of the world was like. But a year or two after the end of the war we took a family trip to Naples to visit my grandmother, whom two of us three children had not yet met. It was our first trip abroad, during the Easter holiday, and it was spellbinding adventure all the way, from the long train ride in a sleeping car with midnight customs procedures to waking up in the morning to a vastly different language and scenery. Not to speak of the white cotton gloves we had to wear, which were gray already in Milan and black by the time we reached Rome. The trains still ran on coal back then, producing an unforgettable, acrid odor, less delicious but just as effective as Proust's over-referenced madeleine, which, truth be told, began its long career as a simple toasted piece of bread before it reached its apotheosis as a biscuit. On the last stretch through Campania we saw water buffaloes grazing in the fields, fleeting impressions lapsing into the past like images on film. Around noon we arrived at the train station called Mergellina, where we were eagerly awaited by my grandmother and her moustached driver Vincenzo. The chaos outside the station, the traffic, the din, the beggars, blind musicians, mutilated veterans, street vendors, palm trees and dilapidated buildings, the filth, the rubble, and the blinding sunlight were unlike anything I had hitherto experienced. Marco Polo cannot have been more stunned by what he saw on the other side of the globe than I was at my first encounter with this foreign country.

After effusive and excited embraces we were packed into the car and chauffeured up the long, winding Corso Vittorio Emanuele to Parco Grifeo—the name of the street where my Nonna had taken up residence again in her home, Villa Lydia, which she had been forced to vacate when the Second World War broke out. The last occupants billeted in that exceptional place were the members of the American command. They must have singled out that splendid villa on account of its prized view of the Bay of Naples: the classical vista of the distant Vesuvius framed by umbrella pines. Its ample grounds were enclosed by a high wall and could easily be spotted from far away, even without binoculars, for they formed the largest patch of green on the built-up hillside. As we drove through the ornate wrought iron gate I noticed several wisterias in bloom. One had clambered up into a tree high above the driveway and diagonally across into the crown of another tree in the most nonchalant way. Such freewheeling behavior would be frowned upon back home. Its rambling manner was as un-Swiss as everything else I had seen so far. Ditto the villa itself—its yellow facade was pock-marked by bullet holes. These were not the only traces the previous occupants had left behind. Inside the house I found wire hangers and stacks of paper cups in a closet: my first and apparently unforgettable introduction to disposable American goods.

The gate at Parco Grifeo 38

Since I was the youngest in the family I spent a lot of time at my grandmother's while my parents and brothers went on excursions. I roamed around the garden, which was a mysterious place, full of deep shade, stone seats, balustrades, and gigantic terracotta pots. As the grounds were asymmetrically terraced on three or four different levels, I was unable to grasp the overall plan. I vaguely remember a grotto which was slightly scary in its sliminess. Further down I encountered a flock of chickens and found them rather incongruous in the elegant atmosphere created by the canopy of pine trees. They were stowaways from the gatekeeper's abode. Dark green foliage, compacted soil, and sculptural elements were the dominant features. When I saw the first saw-edged agave with its sharp points and stiff leaves I could hardly believe that this was a living plant and not an ornament of some inert material, not unlike the miniature metal lamb sitting on a shelf in the guest room we occupied. When on the day of our departure the lamb fell down and broke into pieces, it turned out to be made of chocolate. I had been thoroughly deceived by its iridescent foil wrapping. Naples, famous for its mysteries, works its charm on many levels.Everybody had enormous fun in this garden over the years, grown-ups included. In summertime, lavish dinners for an impressive number of guests were served at a large stone table on the main terrace adjacent to the living room. These sumptuous meals began so late that we children had to sneak out in the dark onto the balcony of the uppermost floor to get a peek at the diners below having their first course served long after our bedtime. The dining and animated chattering often lasted until the wee hours of the morning. Lunch, on the other hand, was invariably served indoors. It was too hot outside and at any rate there was no need to be stingy with daylight or sunshine. There was going to be more of it tomorrow. Lots of it.

Already that first trip to southern Italy changed my perspective forever. I came loose from my moorings and was introduced to what became the leitmotif of my life: feeling simultaneously at home and estranged in another culture. Naples, beyond awakening a desire for adventure, set my inner compass. I began to orient myself towards south like a Muslim locating east before spreading his prayer mat. Manhattan's avenues that run from north to south had such a reassuring effect on me during the first week that I remained in New York for thirty years. I also discovered that New York happens to be on the same latitude as Naples. While the climate of the two cities could not be more different, they share the same strong sunshine, having me suppose that the quality of light must have an influence on our psyche. Just as a determined quantity of sun or shade that plants receive is essential for their wellbeing, similar needs may pertain to humans too.

Villa Lydia

Weather Permitting

Today I am spectacularly, ecstatically happy. It finally rained, two centimeters yesterday and another four last night, after a dry spell that lasted an unusual eight weeks, long before summer began. Every plant all of a sudden looks green and vibrant again, as if nothing had ever been amiss. I luxuriate in the knowledge that I do not have to haul around heavy watering cans and unwieldy hoses for at least another week. The endlessly postponed jobs of seeding and transplanting can be tackled and I plan to get down to some lusty hours of weeding—all tasks that are impossible to perform in our Piacentine hills in northern Italy when drought turns the soil into something resembling cement. Best of all, I also get a break from bending everyone's ear with my obsessive grousing about the harm we have done to the environment and the abysmal future of our planet.

Climate is the theory; weather is what we actually get. Almost everybody has a subjective view on it: the farmer, the balloonist, the beekeeper, even the city dweller who has become hopelessly estranged from country matters, such as that New York cab driver who, during a drought that lowered the city's reservoirs to precarious levels one summer in the 1970s, loudly complained about the lousy climate and, hard to grasp, the excessive rain. Misery has a richer vocabulary than bliss. Amusingly, at the same time Tiffany's on Fifth Avenue displayed a splashing miniature fountain in one of its attractive windows with a notice saying that due to the scarcity of H2O the fountain's liquid had been replaced with pure gin.

I find a certain contentment in the fact that even in our age of advanced physics and technology we cannot predict, much less control, tomorrow's meteorological conditions with certainty. Though we are able to transport ourselves to the moon and communicate with each other from the remotest corners of the globe, the science of how to make the rain fall and the sun shine where we want it still

The Japanese section at Brooklyn Botanical Garden in New York

eludes us. I appreciate this fact as a form of freedom, at least until that is gone too, at which point we will be facing new wars and conflicts about who will direct the sky. Until then we can happily continue to vent our annoyance about the lack of precipitation, the floods, or the exaggerated heat, without aiming our discontent at anyone in particular. Every morning we will come to terms with or prepare for what awaits us outside according to our personal disposition and upbringing. The English butler, upon opening the heavy drapes, greets the guest with a breakfast tray and a

◄◄ The farmer and photographer's idea of
perfect weather: light clouds mixed with sun.

"Lovely gray sky out there," while the Italian maid emphatically exclaims "Che brutto tempo!" when she perceives two solitary clouds in an otherwise blue sky, puts down your double espresso, and suggests you might want to change your plans. But to no one is the weather of more interest than to the avid gardener. He and she grumble about it most days. It seldom is perfect. It is here at the outset that I want to stress an important point: a garden is not a natural occurrence, it is artifice. Horticulture is inclined to foster the rare, which is often synonymous with foreign. For centuries, daring explorers and plant hunters have pried or, more likely, carefully lifted botanical specimens from their native habitat and introduced them to a new location with the desire to make them grow elsewhere. Thus the plants are often put at risk; in their birthplace they seldom get sick or die young. They had millions of years to adapt themselves to freezing temperatures or severe drought or whatever conditions prevail in their place of origin and thus have become biologically programmed to survive these adversities. Not so in the garden, which you could compare to a casino: gambling is going on. This is precisely what makes gardening such an enthralling pastime. A lot of sins are committed in the backyard. Not just in botanical terms, but in esthetic respects too. Most perplexingly, I met some accomplished intellectuals who think of gardens as visually disturbing. After many years of toil and soil I can at least see what they mean although I am not ready to subscribe to their views.

Winter protection for the gazebo is a necessity at
Old Westbury Gardens on Long Island, New York.

Our vineyard in northern Italy benefits from both snow and summer heat.

◄◄ Bougainvillea in Morocco

One thing is clear: it is the climate that deals the cards with which we play the game. Once we get involved in growing plants, learning about their requirements becomes an issue of great interest. This apprenticeship must concern itself first and foremost with local conditions. Temperature, light, water availability, and soil composition determine which plants grow where, and whether a habitat is a marsh or a meadow, a desert or a tropical rainforest. All these factors have to be considered, for there is a lot more to it than geography's roughest division of our planet into three basic zones: arctic, temperate, and tropical. Which is fine for the arctic and the tropical, but insufficient for the temperate zone, where most gardening takes place. There is a cooler and a warmer half of the temperate zone, and many shades in between. The two factors that set the parameters for what we can or cannot grow are frost and drought. Both these conditions are injurious to the cell structure of plants not accustomed to them. Sooner or later they will jeopardize some of your perennials or shrubs. To add to this trouble, the rank beginner often operates under the illusion that he or she will get either frost or drought, but I am sorry to report that it is possible to encounter both of them in one and the same place. As you can guess, I speak from brutal experience. Horticulture is not an exact science but an empirical adventure, and gardeners do not fall from heaven. They too have to learn.

I took my first tentative steps in the cooler half of the temperate zone in America, where I was greatly helped by the hardiness map compiled by the Arnold Arboretum of Harvard University. It slices the continent into ten horizontal zones, which run more or less parallel, except near the coast, where each zone swerves northward, making that particular stretch of land warmer than its neighboring area inland. Proximity to a body of water is a blessing, as it increases the moisture in the air and therefore moderates temperature. Whereas what is known as continental or inland climate denotes the opposite: bigger swings in temperature, colder in winter, hotter in summer, and more so if there is no vegetation. The biggest extremes are found in deserts, where it can become seething hot in sunshine and dip below freezing at night within the same twenty-four hours. The coldest zone, number 1, is uppermost on the map, in Canada. Going down the

A small "garden" shaded
by date palms near the Sahara.

The exuberance of spring is typical for the cooler part of the temperate zone.
Tulip and daffodil bulbs require cold winter temperatures in the ground.

Cherry blossoms ▶

chart, the numbers increase along with the gradual warming of the latitudes. Zone 10 is reached at the southern tip of Florida. Each zone is defined by the minimal annual temperature, by its average temperature, and by its growing days per year. After having absorbed the colorful graphics of this map and pinpointed my whereabouts, I, as an eager novice, did not linger but rushed to consult those useful books in which we can look up to what zone a plant is hardy, that is to say how low the minimum temperature can sink without the cell structure of a given plant breaking down and causing its death. Regrettably this is also where I had to discover that a good number of the plants I yearned to have were not fit to live where I did. If locating yourself on this planet with precision seems too cerebral an approach, let me assure you that where horticulture is concerned, geography is only an approximation with plenty of room for error. Especially since altitude has a say in this equation too. The higher above sea level, the rougher and colder the climate becomes. A 100-meter increase in altitude corresponds to moving northward by 1,000 kilometers (or southward in the southern hemisphere). Which is why it is—or was!—possible to see snowcaps on mountains near the equator. (Due to global warming, Kilimanjaro is about to lose his very soon, and numerous glaciers elsewhere are visibly melting away with increasing speed). This so logical seeming observation we owe to Alexander von Humboldt, the intrepid natural scientist and explorer who set out on long years of perilous travels, cheerfully enduring every conceivable hardship and atrocious food while lugging cumbersome scientific instruments across South American jungles, cataracts, and mountain peaks. He found his true fulfillment in assiduously taking measurements of barometric pressure; the temperature of the water, air, and ground; magnetic fluctuations; and pretty much everything that could be gauged, fathomed, or evaluated. Most importantly, he took astrological sightings of his position wherever he went, fixed latitudes and longitudes, set records straight, and established new maps. In short, he brought order and precision to geography. What is more, he recorded all his findings in a waterproof ink he had invented, thanks to which his notes survived a shipwreck on the Orinoco and numerous other accidents. It is odd that

▲ Unsettled weather at Lamb House in Rye, England

34

this happened a mere 200 years ago. Today we can cull our exact position at any given moment on the navigator screen of our car. I stare at it in amazement and think of the 100,000 vicious insect bites and grueling misadventures Humboldt and his companion Bonpland suffered in their keen pursuit of science.

In upstate New York, near Millbrook in Dutchess County, where we built a house, a vital question was how low the beastly winter temperature could fall without posing a risk to the trees and shrubs we hoped to plant. A stroll in the neighborhood gave us a fair idea of what could be grown with success. But to my initial consternation I found out that not even fundamental furnishings such as box and roses would safely make it through the cold season in zone 4. Winter protection is a major preoccupation where subzero temperatures prevail and where the ground freezes for long stretches of time. Mulching can lessen the damage of temperature changes, as it prevents the heaving of plants caused by repeated freezing and thawing. Novices may think that mulch keeps the soil warm. But it does the opposite: it keeps the ground cold and hinders the roots from working themselves to the surface. By far the best insulation is snow. You don't have to buy it, spread it, or remove it, and it does not attract mice. Unfortunately, it did not always arrive, and I covered the ground with evergreen boughs from other people's Christmas trees since we always planted

Rain again? At New College in Oxford

our own. There are other ways of protection, such as keeping the soil heaped over as much of the plant as possible where that is feasible. It is all a question of how maniacal we want to become. Gardening is definitely a magnet for the obsessively inclined. Of course, every place has its own characteristics, its exposed areas, its niches and protected corners. In the latter you might get away with planting a specimen that is only marginally hardy in your region. Come November you can give it some winter protection by wrapping it in burlap or plastic. This I did, with the former, but after one or two tries of the sort I felt this was where gardening stopped being fun, especially when after removing the wrapping too soon I ended up with casualties from a late spring frost, which is when most damage happens. In my seventeen

years of American gardening I accumulated quite a few such sorry incidents, first through ignorance and later through misguided perseverance. I finally gave in when I witnessed how it took the decimated *Daphne mezereum* or the ruined *Santolina rosmarinifolia* all spring and half the summer to recover from winter burn, when I could have gotten many more months of pleasure out of a homelier, native plant. It is a better policy to start with the easy or mundane. Ambition and sophistication can come later.

Winter's biggest asset is that it is followed by spring. No other season can boast such a shining light at the end of the tunnel. The awakening of nature, when the buds swell and the earliest blossoms pop, almonds first, then apricots and cherries, their fragile blooms bravely standing up to the sometimes still chilly nights, is indisputably the year's most exhilarating moment. Every day we find tender green spears pushing up from the dark, moist soil where two weeks earlier we could have sworn that nothing was happening underneath because we had simply forgotten the spot where we planted some bulbs. Well-defined seasons are the mark of the temperate zone, where deciduous trees and shrubs shed their leaves when the plants go to sleep, suspending all operations for a good long while, only to make a comeback in spring, dependably starting the cycle anew with unstinting generosity and vigor. Were I to live in the arctic or in the tropics, I would surely be driven to drink due to the monotony of nature's unaltered scenery. Movement and change are at the core of our existence, and new is therefore what we crave. If only I could reduce the tyranny of winter to an intense but brief period of four or five weeks...

▲ *Sanguinaria canadensis* "Duplex" Schloss Bothmar in Malans, Switzerland ▶
is blessed by a microclimate.

Agapanthus can stay in the ground all year in the warmer part of the temperate zone.

The ecstasy of spring is made even more pronounced by the looming possibility of a relapse into winter, which could bring wrack and ruin. At the war museum in Tokyo I found myself standing in front of a wooden case—like the ones we know from butterfly collections—divided into eight or nine compartments, each of which displayed a different species of Japanese cherry blossom. It was a most unexpected object in the midst of nasty weaponry and cruel photographs. To Western sensibility it seems too big a leap from kamikaze to the fragile blooms of sato-sakura, but in Tokyo it makes its point: the cherry blossom is Japan's symbol for the soldier's brief life. While frost is a normal occurrence during the winter in temperate zones, in spring it becomes an insidious enemy. Its glacial hand causes devastating damage, likely to kill off all buds and tender seedlings in a few hours. Not a pretty sight, and quite unlike the autumnal hoarfrost with its sparkling crystals on the leaves and berries of mature plants. Moreover, we can accept autumn's happenings as the natural progression of time. Most disconcertingly, spring frost is known to strike out of the blue, and quite literally so: clear skies increase the probability of its occurrence, as do cool temperatures and the absence of wind. Anthropomorphic thinking somehow gets in the way when help could be given.

For who would readily resort to grabbing a garden hose on a freezing morning to wash down the young buds or recently set out seedlings with a stream of cold water? The mere idea makes me shiver, yet it is the correct thing to do. For water, no matter how cold, melts away the ice that begins to form on stems and leaves, thus giving the young plants another chance. It is a question of physics and not of warm-blooded intuition.

Frost, that uninvited guest, does not necessarily show up in every part of the garden. For there is such a phenomenon as a microclimate, that is to say a defined area which can be either blessed or cursed, with weather conditions that differ from the adjacent terrain. A sunny, sheltered wall can create a microclimate for instance, as does the vicinity of a body of water. Being on a hillside also can turn out to be an advantage, not just on account of summer breezes but because it gives frost the opportunity to roll down and away. By pure chance we benefit from such a situation in the foothills of the Apennines, while gardens in the Po Valley, just

Early morning frost threatens the almond blossoms.

The humidity is palpable on Martha's Vineyard between the seashore and a pond.

a few miles away, are hopelessly socked in and regularly suffer frost damage. This is easier to understand once we comprehend that frost behaves exactly like water. When it cannot go any further, it accumulates. I visited a walled garden in England on sloping land, within which the morning frost regularly got trapped. This condition was remedied as if by magic when its owner made a door-sized opening in the lower wall, through which the cold air took French leave when no longer halted by a solid barrier. Mystics call this Feng Shui, but again, it's simply physics.

When we have the cold spells behind us, another unpredictable fellow makes his unwanted appearance in our region: wind. If frost follows the behavior of water, then wind has to be compared to sound. It races, whirls around, ricochets, and can reach us from a perfectly unexpected angle, the way an echo or a billiard ball does. But even when it is the straightforward kind, it is a major enemy of plants. And I don't mean gales that uproot trees, but just plain everyday wind. Even at a normal rate it retards or stunts a plant's growth. I planted five crab apple trees in a row, all the same size, whereof three are protected by a wall at their back. The two in a more open position were already lagging behind in their development a year later because some of their energy must have gone into battling the wind. The baffling effect of aerodynamics was demonstrated even more clearly by an *Arbutus unedo* (strawberry tree) that I placed in a very protected spot in the corner of our south-facing terrace. After a ferocious storm, it presented us with hopelessly wind-burnt branches, not as one would expect at its front, but hidden near the wall in the back. Physics never ceases to surprise me. Southern Europe is well known for its unpopular winds that often come up when nature is already stressed by drought, which undoubtedly adds to the mistral's and scirocco's bad press. The Swiss foehn also has the ability to frazzle people's nerves, even those of townspeople who do not own plants.

My husband and I were congratulating ourselves to have lucked out with our Italian find, having landed on a spot which in winter is often above the sea of fog

The desert garden at Jardin Majorelle in Marrakech is dry, dry, dry.

our region is famous for. It also offers pleasant summer temperatures, which we had hoped for but could not take for granted. But what we had not expected was the prevailing wind coming up from the Mediterranean coast. When it reaches its maximum strength I feel that we plunked ourselves down onto one of the major wind paths of Europe. In a more confined area one would consider putting up a windbreak with a belt of trees that could withstand these assaults. But being on a promontory and open to the valley, this is not feasible. Add to this that the rainclouds chasing up from Genoa hit the southwestern side of the Apennines first, where they unload their contents. By the time they reach our horizon they are often out of funds and we barely get a sprinkle. So drought and wind are the downside of our little Arcadia. However, even if we had known about them, we would still have chosen the same place. Gradually one comprehends that almost all situations have their plusses and minuses. The wind and the breezes that in spring are distinctly unwelcome, later in the season not only refresh body and soul but so far also have kept mosquitos and mildew away. So we go with the flow.

But the fat end is to follow. For as if it is not daunting enough to gauge the parameters of what can safely be planted in our gardens, the unpredictable dynamics of climate change have put a more threatening wrench into the works. True, the weather has always been known for its vicissitude. Severe droughts, record rainfalls, devastating storms, and hurricanes have been visited upon mankind all along but I can see clearly that now they arrive at shorter intervals and hit with increased force. "Global warming" is just part of the problem. The new reality is that climate stability and predictable seasons have been obliterated and what we henceforth can count on is the weather's increasingly erratic behavior everywhere. Or as I saw written on a wall in Milan: "The future is no longer what it used to be."

Unprecedented: The black cloud that didn't give us a drop of rain.

Unprecedented: The hailstorm that bashed my watermelon.

The Schinz family on holiday

Carl von Linne's garden ins Uppsala

In the south,

Ginevra and Mathilde Buchy with their guardian
and their cousins in Sarno near Naples

As a lover of heat, the south had much more influence on my life than the north, or the pull between east and west. I am by no means the only one: the lure of the Mediterranean basin has been irresistible to many, and the spell that Italy casts on northerners goes back many centuries. Originally the attraction was due to the riches of the Italian Renaissance. If some of that flowering culture was due to the climate I cannot answer. Many European painters and poets followed their inner call to spend time in Italy. Goethe for one, officially the greatest writer of the German language and also a worthy naturalist, rhapsodized not only of dark-eyed girls but of sweet-scented lemon groves as well. He paid thorough attention to and studied the world of plants, while Chaucer, who had no botanical knowledge as such, could not help but notice the size and health of Italian hollies 400 years earlier. And when in the more recent past travel increased, English, Russian, and German denizens of the leisure class flocked to Italy to spend the winter in Tuscany, intent on evading the rigorous climate of their fatherlands. Madame Lucy de la Tour du Pin wrote in 1842 that warming one's bones in Italy felt like pouring oil on a rusty old lock. It is a recipe that still works.

The music thus elicited by the cord that has been strung from north to south reverberates in my blood too, as my ancestors straddle the divide of the Alps. My paternal roots are in Switzerland, while my mother's forbears hail from Naples. Both strains and both climates left their unmistakable imprint on my temperament. Arduously conquering mountains with walking sticks and great determination was my Swiss ancestors' idea of a holiday. Whereas leisure, fun, and posing for photographs in the shade of palm trees and umbrella pines was how my grandmother passed her summers in southern Italy. The Swiss virtues of moderation, industry, and self-restraint are in constant dialogue if not downright combat with the leisurely attitude, cordial effusiveness, and baroque excess of the south. Neapolitan hedonism has been grafted onto Swiss sobriety.

The way out of climate restrictions is having ▶
a greenhouse. This is at the *vivaio* of Anna
and Saskia Peyron in Castagneto, near Turin.

My Good Earth

Once the temptation to grow something has become irrepressible, we need soil. Its function is to hold a plant in its place and supply it with the elements necessary to its growth. The soil is probably already in your backyard or, if you only have a balcony or a window box, you may have to buy growing medium or potting soil in plastic bags. These products—irony aside—have more air in them than the compacted ground in your backyard, unless the latter has been dug up recently. How important the air content of the soil is cannot be emphasized enough: it is the be-all and end-all of gardening. Whatever kind of soil we are dealing with, it could be compared to women's hair: rarely perfect, there is no limit to the grooming and conditioning that can be applied to improve its original state. Soil is usually improved by adding certain substances, and every gardening manual encourages you to enrich your own by digging in humus and manure until its consistency can be compared to crumbling chocolate cake. This is definitely easier said than done because I could never buy humus, nor is well-rotted manure readily available. It is much simpler to buy chocolate cake.

There is a lot more to this substance we call soil than meets the eye. I am talking about the uppermost layer of earth known as topsoil, which in America is also—and incomprehensibly—called "dirt." Ideally topsoil should be three feet deep, but I cannot remember ever having seen that. In reality it is more like one or maximum two feet deep. Topsoil is made up of ground rock, decayed vegetable waste, water, and air. The proportion of these ingredients varies from one place to the next. It was originally formed by our planet's bare rock becoming pulverized by eons of abrasive weather, changes in temperature, advancing and retreating glaciers, and so on. Then by some mysterious and for us incredible stroke of luck, cell dividing organisms were born. Algal cells, fungi, mosses, and lichens began to establish themselves among the rocks. Millennia later, bacteria joined the process, feeding on those composite organisms and provoking their decay, a process through which soil started to form and build up. All this happened excruciatingly slowly,

Mosses and lichens appeared on our planet 250 million
years ago. The human face arrived many, many eons later.

but eventually, that is to say many zeros later, our biosphere came into existence.
Most of us don't think very highly of such lowly forms of life as the likes of lichens.
Lichens rank lower than ferns on the evolutionary scale, but at least they are one
step up from fungi and algae. Even though the poor things are rootless, stemless,
flowerless, and leafless, they are nevertheless worthy of our attention. One kind in
particular has my full approval. I am talking about Iceland moss, *Cetraria islandica*,
which I knew from my childhood in the form of an opaque, beige cough drop
with an intriguing flavor and a porous texture that allowed me to suck it into slimy
foam real fast. Later on, I had occasion to observe its role in the manufacturing of

My first garden in Katonah

marbled papers. Other lichens are called upon by artisans for equally specialized tasks, as dyes in the manufacture of Harris Tweed or to create miniature plants for architectural models. Lichens are also an indicator of a pollution-free environment. Fifty million years of usefulness is definitely food for thought, and wouldn't it be a fine idea to point out to the unsuspecting young that often there are substantial riches stored under the wrinkly surface of old age?

The first time I actually put a spade in the ground was shortly after we got married. No surprise this—the onset of gardening quite naturally coincides with settling down and acquiring some land of one's own. We had found and bought a wonderfully elegant place in Katonah, New York, an hour's drive north of Manhattan. A short driveway lined with giant old maple trees led to the white colonial house and its stable, crowned by a turret, for which we were going to get a pair of white doves. We purchased them and in less than a year they interbred with ugly city pigeons and produced totally unwanted offspring. Thereafter we acquired a cat, hoping she would deal with the pigeons, which she did. Ancient apple trees were scattered throughout the lawns and fields surrounding the complex of buildings. It was a picture of perfection, a green and white American dream. In order not to jeopardize such immaculate beauty I had selected a spot out of sight, between an old stone-wall and a horse fence, where I could risk failure with a first experiment. Combing through various nurseries I had been able to locate a basil plant in a six-inch pot, a rarity in those pre-culinary-revolution days, and brought it to my chosen strip of land. Without much ado I removed some grass, dug up the soil, stuck in my plant, watered it, and watched it grow until it was time to turn it into pesto. This easy success spurred me on to increase my efforts. The following year I doubled my basil holdings, bought six young tomato plants, and surrounded them with nasturtiums from one of those pretty little seed packets. It all grew beautifully, and I was hooked.

Every year I opted for a new feature. I learned about railway ties and decided on the advantages of raised beds. For these I bought some extra soil from a nurseryman who unloaded a truck full of what he proudly pronounced to be the best stuff in the county, coming from a former greenhouse no longer in use. Unfortunately, it turned out to also contain zillions of shards of glass. Pretty ghastly. I painstakingly sifted these out for days on end while trying to familiarize myself with the costly substance that was going to bring me closer to perfection. It was an introduction to

Breaking ground

Every gardener's dream: a huge pile of humus

pure Americana, from the railway ties to the idea of buying soil and being bamboo-
zled in the process. Not to speak of the fact that a large area of my growing empire
had to be cleared of poison ivy, another American novelty to me, far more danger-
ous than the nettles of my youth. But nothing marred my delight of seeing things
flourish, and I kept adding, another bed here, a perennial border there, a proper
compost corner, and finally an electric fence to protect my precious improvements
from the ever-encroaching herds of deer. It was an unpretentious patch of land you
might compare to a needlepoint sampler, where climate and soil provided the warp
and the woof for the canvas of my first horticultural embroideries.

Simultaneously I became a voracious reader of various garden manuals and catalogs, and of Rodale's *Organic Gardening* magazine, which originally was published in a
conveniently small format like *Reader's Digest*, and could be leafed through with moist
hands while soaking in a hot bathtub after a day of backbreaking labor. James Under-
wood Crockett's *Victory Garden* book—a spin-off of his TV show—saw me through the
ABC of growing vegetables, while the Czech writer Karel Čapek kept me in stitches
about the comical aspects of the impassioned gardener. The *Wise Garden Encyclopedia*

was the bible on my night table. I consulted it at dawn and dusk just as insatiably as my husband went through his stacks of *The Blood-Horse* magazine. My appetite steadily grew despite the fact that every plant entry in some of my books ended in lengthy paragraphs about its subject's enemies and diseases. Clearly, gardening was not for the lazy or the depressed. Miki Denhoff, the editor at *House and Garden*, who gave me my first assignments and with whom I occasionally exchanged horticultural insights, suggested to me in her memorably accented voice that I should simply skip over the discouraging bits. I was stunned. We were dealing with national differences here. I was Swiss and did not, could not, was not allowed to skip. She was of Viennese origin, which implied a certain largesse and waltzing flexibility. Only a lifetime later, when consulting the *Merck Manual* became a necessary evil, did I get the hang of skipping. Ignorance is bliss. Why focus on all manners of death when we will fall prey to only one.

Good earth, as I soon witnessed, is of capital importance to the health of vegetation. There are different types of soils. It is the composition of the original mother rock that determines what will result from its disintegration. Limestone ends up as clay soil; granite, gneiss, and sandstone tend toward sandy and somewhat more acidic soils. The size of its particles also matters. Soil texture is classifiable and ranges from coarse gravel to the finest of silt. These particles are key to the soil's behavior, for instance regarding its draining ability or lack thereof, that is to say how porous it is by providing tiny spaces for air. But whatever the basic character of the soil, it is humus, that delicious, brown, fluffy, sweet-smelling stuff that will supply most of what our soil may be missing. Formed by decayed plant and animal substances and teeming with microorganisms, it improves the texture of the earth, making it spongy and water retentive without becoming waterlogged. If made properly it also supplies some nutrients and boosts growth; in short, it is the time-honored panacea for all soils and many plants. Before chocolate cake invaded horticultural vernacular, the most desirable stuff was called loam. Rich loam is what every gardener is striving for in order to create a beneficial environment to make his or her garden happy, healthy, and productive.

There is no garden writer who has not sung the praise of compost making and, indeed, once you get the stuff to properly morph it does work wonders. But it is not usually there when you start a garden as the carefully saved kitchen scraps, untainted by salt, sugar, oil, meat, milk, or cheese never amount to much unless you have a restaurant. It took me at least two years of gardening to build a very small pile of discarded weeds, stalks, and grass clippings. Do not believe anyone telling you that after the first year you will find the black gold you aspire to. And though

I encouraged even the most distinguished house guests to go and micturate on or at the compost heap, I am embarrassed to admit that despite such valuable additions of nitrogen my pile never heated up the way it does in instruction manuals. It takes patience, like all of gardening. But it is certainly worthwhile to plug away at it. It also makes life easier in the kitchen. There is never a moment's hesitation about which salad leaves to discard and which to eat. Dust to dust and ashes to ashes, and less than pristine vegetables onto the compost heap. Some subjects such as overgrown zucchinis go there directly without an intermediary stop in the kitchen or, God forbid, at the table. In other words, composting has a fringe benefit: it reduces guilt.

From my garden literature I gathered that topsoil is not only the carrier of water and nutrients, but that in addition it has its pH value (acid, neutral, or alkaline), which can be of importance. This was chemistry, which has always appealed to me more than physics. I could not wait to buy a soil testing kit at a well-stocked garden center and subsequently was able to determine that my soil was slightly acid: pH factor 6.8. I was a little taken aback. Acid did not have a good sound to me. But help was within reach, and it was relatively inexpensive: sprinkling powdered lime over the freshly dug plot to neutralize the acidity was easy and fun, and spreading ashes from our fireplace on the veg patch in spring proved to be even more satisfying since I have always had a flirt with self-sufficiency. Tampering with the soil suited my temperament and I got deeper and deeper into improvements.

At some point I hit on a brilliant idea. Our three horses and our donkey had conventional straw bedding in their stalls, which when mucked out took much too long to decompose. This seemed a darned shame, and when I discovered that friends of ours had brown rice hulls as bedding, I felt that this was the solution I should be angling for. Once they had served in the stable they could be dug under in the garden and make life easier for my plants. Luckily I was able to convince my ever-willing husband to put an end to straw and try rice hulls instead. It took a while to find a source, which eventually was located in another state, and so the hulls had to be trucked to us from hundreds of miles away. The shipment arrived, a few hours earlier than anticipated, and when we got home from our daily commute we beheld a bewildering sight. In our absence the truck had dumped twenty huge packs of about five cubic feet each in front of our driveway. The hulls were neither in cardboard boxes nor in sacks, but merely encased in brown wrapping paper. Some of them had ripped open, oozing rice hulls which, horror of horrors, were not luscious brown but bleached white. Wind had come up in the mean-

Right time, right place

A woman's work is never done.

Well rotted manure is waiting to be spread in a French potager.

A young woman near Hanoi prepares a seed bed for rice, which will get dusted with ashes.

time and had already blown some of the stuff all over the place. It was ghastly. Why would anyone bleach rice hulls? Why had we not been told? And what was this lousy packing job? I pulled out my hair and felt like sinking into the ground for having caused such a mess, but what did not sink into the ground were the rice hulls. No matter how often I tried to dig them under, they drifted back to the surface with every rain and round of watering. To make the measure full, they looked like maggots but had the longevity of plastic. As I now know they consist of lignin and are extremely slow to decompose, even slower than straw, so I ran afoul of the composting idea too. They never did anything good, did not lighten the soil nor enrich the ground. The horses did not

mind them, but in the final analysis they merely drove home the point that gardening is empirical in nature and comes with the risk of trial and horrendous error. The rice hulls took about five years to disappear from sight, but my soil got better all the time in spite of them. Digging, hoeing, weeding, fertilizing are all actions that benefit the ground, a process further enhanced and promoted by the roots of whatever is growing. Another addition to the process is also made by the praiseworthy travails of earthworms, who act as small soil refineries. Growing potatoes is an excellent idea when starting a new garden, as the earth gets constantly moved around, not only when planting and harvesting but also by the ceaseless push applied by the tubers themselves. Or we can follow Sir Peter Smithers' example, who planted a bleak hillside near Lake Lugano with camellias and magnolias and left their spent thick leaves and blossoms on the ground to decompose and become soil.

Just when my soil seemed to near its ideal state, something rather unexpected happened. We moved. What is more, we moved in the wrong direction. We moved north. Of course I was going to have a garden. I decidedly was still enamored of soil improvement and have remained so. First there were large pebbles and small rocks to be removed, which worked themselves to the surface every year. Compared to the rice hulls and the shards of glass in Katonah this was a cinch, indeed a pleasurably childish task. During the 1980s the general interest in gardening was on a healthy rise in the United States. Nurseries and garden centers became better stocked with offerings of hitherto unknown materials. In an attempt to get closer to the chocolate cake consistency touted in garden articles I treated myself to dozens of bags of dark brown cocoa hulls, which I spread in some places as mulch and elsewhere dug under to lighten the soil. They smell delicious, decompose fast, and enrich the ground effectively. At about that time I also wrote a letter to the Bronx Zoo to ask if I could buy elephant dung from them—a pad would go a long way—and fantasized that lion droppings might turn out to be a potent deer repellent. Needless to say that in my mind's eye I saw these exotic excrements imaginatively packaged with first-rate graphics and appealing woodblock print decorations. Alas, I was reaching for the moon. I got a disappointing letter back saying that the sanitation department would not stand for such practices. With the increasing sophistication of the American gardening public, better and rarer plants became available from both nurseries and catalog houses. Whatever I bought or sent for, I obediently paid attention to my pH value of 6.8, sprinkling lime only when necessary on vegetable beds, but otherwise limiting my choice of plants to those that would tolerate slightly acid soil. And so my garden became richer and more

Rich loamy soil in Devon

Sandy soil in North Africa

luxuriously furnished every year and soon was to reach its apotheosis. Maybe the reader is familiar with a board game named snakes and ladders, where little ladders give the player a jump up, while snakes set him back. At the next to last square on number 99 of our board lurked a snake the size of a boa constrictor that put the doomed player back to the beginning in one fell swoop. This is exactly what happened to my gardening. I took a giant leap back to square one. Because we moved again. This time it was a radical change. As our children had flown the coop and my husband was no longer allowed to ride horses, we phased out our place in Dutchess County and started to look for a villa in Italy. After a lengthy search we found a *casa padronale* in Emilia, the large region between Lombardy and Tuscany, south of the River Po. The attractive house and its farm buildings sat on a promontory in the hilly countryside surrounded by fairly steep farmed fields. This fine spot had been selected around 1600 by a gentleman who knew what he was after. Breathtaking views of farmland, vineyards, and woods made the place too good to be true. The spirit of the landscape spoke to us. It spoke to us in Italian about beauty, *villegiatura*, and the pleasures of country living.

Clayish soil in my neighborhood in Italy

Though the fields looked very handsome, soil erosion on steep terrain is inevitable and had already taken its toll: the local farmers' crops were meager. When I tried to stick my spade into the ground, I couldn't. It was hard as rock, baked by the harsh sun of endless summers. Having picked up a nugget of soil the size of a walnut, I moistened it, rolled it in my hand, then flattened it, thinner and thinner, like pastry dough. It showed my fingerprint in detail—the proof of its high clay content. At that instant I knew that I should have subscribed to pottery instead of gardening. But plants were needed more than pots, so I had to begin again from scratch. Clay soil is notoriously difficult to cultivate. It is slippery when wet, hard when dry, and takes a long time to become workable in spring. Woe is you if you dig it too soon. Cementlike clods will be the result, which neither chisel nor hammer can pry apart, and I am not kidding. Only exposure to hard frost breaks up these clods, which is why the drought-prone fields that surround me now depend on freezing winters to do their work. True, clayish soil holds moisture better than sandy soil, but it also has the nasty habit of shrinking when it dries out, forming deep cracks, the size of which indicate how long there has been no precipitation.

The air mentioned at the beginning of this chapter was by no means just a jocular utterance. It is the clay soil's compactness that interferes with the oxygen supply to the roots of the plants. I was flabbergasted when, at the beginning of our Italian life, a man who brought some bushes for our initial foundation planting suggested we should first have the soil and the subsoil near the buildings broken up—get this—with a pneumatic drill. How unromantic. No wonder I became a dormant hortophile after that. Luckily I woke up from my Cinderella nap a few years later, when I worked on a photographic portrait of a garden in Tuscany and suddenly understood the fertile nature of clay soil, provided we choose plants equipped to deal with the difficult ground. It is no terrain for milquetoasts. Sturdy plants with strong roots such as fig trees, pomegranates, grapevines, cherry laurels, lavender, irises, and roses not only do well but actually thrive—provided they get enough rain. With this new insight I was swayed to go back to proper gardening.

A plowed field nearby

Winter freezes make my clayish ▶
clods of soil burst into layers.

The interim years we had spent on planting trees, to give shape and shade to the terrain surrounding the house. Some of them had found an underground vein of water and were growing faster than others. But gardening cannot be left to chance. Plenty of organic matter of any kind was needed—spent hops, peanut shells, algae, leaf mold, mushroom compost—but none of these recommendable soil improvers could be found. There were no nurseries of quality nearby. We were among farmers, whose wives had little time to grow flowers and were content with the inevitable red geraniums and a few roses. Six-packs of petunias in mixed colors and frequently mislabeled vegetable seedlings were the typical offering at local feed stores or at the weekly markets. The more distinguished nurseries were far away, in Tuscany, the cradle of everything including arborists and the nursery trade.

No matter how much organic stuff I added to my soil, nothing had a lasting impact. Whatever I did, within twelve months or so it reverted to its former churlish self, making me feel like Sisyphus himself. Despite my manifold efforts, quite a number of the small plants I bought in pots went into a rapid decline once in the ground and became smaller every week, then disappeared completely. Initially I attributed the cause to the soil being too alkaline, a condition exacerbated by the frequent lack of rain. But when no fertilizer or magic potions helped, I began to understand that the problem was not one of chemistry but of mechanics. Plants started in pots in a soft growing medium have fine roots and cannot hack it when suddenly surrounded by stiffer soil, which they are unable to penetrate. Even the proverbial one-dollar hole for a ten-cent plant did not work, because it gets the roots only so far. Finally, only when I resorted to adding sand—river sand to be sure, not builder's sand, which would have made the catastrophe complete—did things begin to look up. Many shrubs took a leap forward, and even some smaller perennials such as the intensely blue flowered *Ceratostigma plumbaginoides* and the *Epimedium pinnatum* began to multiply and conquer new territory as they are supposed to. As did a single sprig of a silver-edged groundelder, which had literally stayed put for twelve years without ever budging. It suddenly took off with boundless enthusiasm, giving proof that the right kind of friable soil is the main road to success.

▲ Potting soil resembling chocolate cake.

In all these toils I was never alone. Several characters kept me company in the background. First, there was Jacob from the Old Testament, with his seven-year servitude for what turned out to be the wrong bride (Katonah), and seven more for Rachel, a marriage that ended too soon (Millbrook). Later in Italy, where I wrestle with our intractable soil, Arthur Schopenhauer kicks in and whispers in my ear: "Fool that you are—did I not underline that there is no bigger misfortune than to overlook happiness when you have it at your fingertips! Why were you not content with your pH value of 6.8?" So I reconcile myself with my soil and currently find encouragement in Picasso's remark: "What keeps me working today is the notion that tomorrow I'll be worse."

Pierino is optimistically looking into
the future on a mountain of cow manure.

Plowing and seeding is still done the biblical way in Morocco.

The Rake's
Slow Progress

When deliberating whether it was gardening or agriculture that made its entry first into our history, I have no doubt that it was gardening: the delightful pursuit of beauty. As my imagination turns to the cool mists of time, I envision our prehistoric ancestor returning from a successful hunt and throwing his kill—a reindeer perhaps—onto a rock, content to have secured a few juicy meals, when he perceives a single, wonderful flower near the entrance to his cave. Poetic license permits me to suggest it was a poppy, maybe even a blue Himalayan poppy, that most spellbinding of flowers, breathtaking to look at and— 14,000 years later—given the name *Meconopsis betonicifolia*. My *Homo sapiens* calls out for his female companion, and they both gaze in awe at the pure sky-blue blossom. In order to see it better, they liberate it from some grasses that grow near it, and scratch around its base with a stone wedge. They relish the sight every day, and may have had some regrets when the last bloom was gone. Life went on as usual, and the following year not one flower sprang up in the same spot, but three, and a whole slew more a few steps away. It was the Golden Age of humanity. There was enough game and food around for everybody, and gathering provided just the right amount of entertainment and exercise. Nobody was obese, or even overweight, and nobody had to go to the gym. Then it all changed. God was introduced, and He in turn invented Adam and Eve, who were pushed into agriculture and the therewith connected struggles and necessities. Life became more complicated, even if seemingly securer. Suddenly there were obligations to be met, deadlines to be kept; arguments arose and accusations were batted back and forth.

What is sure is that our Stone Age forbears were sharp observers of plant and animal life and in close touch with nature at all times. They probably had blue fingers from picking bilberries. Having a "green thumb" is not a mystical gift, but a metaphor for our willingness to look at a plant and respond to its needs. The

◄ At Quinta da Bacalhôa in Portugal

This storage room with tools south of Naples
probably looked just the same 2,000 years ago.

pleasure we get from a plant's reaction to our nurturing efforts is the very essence of gardening. Once we have experienced the satisfaction of seeing a flowering shrub perk up in the summer heat after we have given it a good long soaking, or when witnessing the blooming gratitude of a patch of flowers following an application of lovingly prepared manure tea, we find ourselves embarked on a new reciprocal relationship. Call it a green thumb if you wish; it is a thumb used to work hand in glove with nature. My best garden gloves, by the way, are made in Vietnam. They are rubbery and white and indestructible, and when I slip them on I instantly feel transformed and ready to take on any task. Especially weeding.

For weed we must. It is the most basic of tasks and a chore we await like the refrain in a song. Since the garden is the place we set apart from the wilderness so as to grow the plants we favor, we must edit nature by eliminating whatever interferes with the picture we are trying to create. We pull out the plants that grow out of place and which we therefore call weeds. But weeds are a man-made prejudice and a controversial subject. The farmer or the horticulturalist does not tolerate them in the place they choose for themselves. He is vexed by the most tenacious among them and would not give a damn if burdocks, thistles, brambles, couch grass, and bindweed did not exist at all. The botanist is at odds with this view. His role is all-embracing and democratic. For her or him, a weed per se does not exist. If pressed to define the aforementioned transgressors as a group, he might do so as a group of stalwart survivors of uncommon vitality, with a ferocious desire to live and multiply, usually at the expense of others, by some deemed worthier plants. If their merit has not been found yet, it probably will be in the future.

Dandelion, that tough weed, is a good example of lopsided calumny. For *Taraxacum officinale*, its proper Latin name, is endowed with many beneficial properties, a fact we can deduct from the "officinale" on its label. It is a treasure trove of proteins, sugars, minerals, vitamins, wax, latex, as well as active ingredients like alkaloids, glycosides, and tannins. Known as a health plant to the Arab physician Avicenna in the eleventh century, it has been portrayed in European herbals many times. Its leaves can be eaten raw or cooked, its juice extracted to make dandelion tea, its roots chopped, roasted, and ground to make dandelion coffee. Its flowers are rich in nectar and attract bees in large numbers. And as if that were not enough, its familiar fluffy ball of seeds is the delight of every child. That same seed ball has also been appropriated by Larousse, the French publisher of encyclopedias, as a symbol for the dissemination of knowledge. And long before that, dandelions, with their unmistakable silhouette, found their way into the design of millefleur tapestries and paintings. Weed? I cannot think of a plant that has more to recommend itself. There are also newer intruders of a similar twofold reputation. The ornamental water hyacinth, for instance, became an invasive pest shortly after it was introduced to tropical waterways, where

An ornament at Hall Barn in Buckinghamshire

it chokes out the endemic flora of rivers and lakes. Modern studies of that greedy but pretty chap have led to new findings, and *Eichhornia crassipes* can now be put to work to decontaminate polluted ground. Some members of the grass family also have their negative side and are perforce regarded as the nemesis of lawns. Crab grass, for instance, was held in high regard by lake dwellers in Neolithic Switzerland, who grew it as a grain crop. And couch grass, a leading thug and unflappable underground agent, was recommended by Culpeper, the physician and herbalist, as a cure for kidney ailments. More recently, quack grass (*Agropyron repens*), another invader, has become an amusing pawn in the hands of my friends Mary and Craig. Every year they invite their neighbors over to a weeding party, and the person who extracts the longest intact rope of root wins a prize. The longest measured so far was six feet. Many other "weeds" provide habitats and food for insects and birds, and a great many of them, including nettles, earned their keep as pot herbs and suppliers of ancient pharmaceutica. As you have already guessed: the list of so-called weeds with useful properties can be extended almost indefinitely. To boot, they all prevent soil erosion and manufacture oxygen. So in the world at large there is no such thing as a weed, whereas in our garden we are king and decide over all our subjects, as absolute rulers or benevolent dictators as the case may be, beheading, extracting, burning, or simply digging under the wild plants we do not want to have around.

I once watched an accomplished English gardener absorbed in weeding and could not help asking him if he liked what he was doing. Yes, he said, it's such a mindless task. Therein lies the therapy of gardening. You can think your own thoughts. Or you can advertise them. My father's passion was botany, and nothing made him happier than a daily tour of the garden in the company of one of us children. Every so often he would bend down, embonpoint notwithstanding, and pull out a weed in his path with exclamations of "Écrasez l'infâme!" He was mentally addressing his opponents in the Kantonsrat (the cantonal legislative assembly) or his enemies within the medical faculty; both were institutions that provided plenty of friction and procured the opportunity of sublimation by weeding. I too like weeding, and sometimes get an urge to indulge in the close encounters with those pernicious agents to work off other annoyances. This was easy on my friable American soil and possible at any given moment. But in my garden in the Piacentino hills I sometimes have to wait for weeks until the conditions are just right: humid but not wet, and above all not too dry, for then all you do is rip off the green tops—the weeds' better halves so to speak. Ordinarily I prefer to wait until they have reached a certain size so that when they are extracted the soil gets moved around and aired. In the meantime they keep the ground shaded—a plus in a sunny climate. Of course,

An allotment gardener in Ljubljana, Slovenia ▶

I have developed personal relationships with these non-ornamentals too. On the personable side we find chickweed, purslane, lamb's quarters, and Good King Henry, all of which are edible should you be infatuated with the notion of food from the wild (which I am not). Chickweed is particularly pretty and tender, and springs up just about everywhere as soon as the weather turns cool. I enjoy its bright green color. My fabulous gloves that snugly fit my hands give me a strong grip. They prevent grasses from slipping through my fingers and make clawing around deep down in the soil very effective when I try to locate the roots of bindweed, for instance. If I cannot get them out with my hands alone, I resort to a three-pronged hoe with a short handle and go after them like Captain Hook, on my knees, determined to let nobody escape, for the tiniest bit of root left in the soil has the ability to regenerate and does so with a vengeance. These aggressive individuals, by the way, should not go on the compost heap but be condemned to die by fire. I usually fall short of this goal, and since the sun dries out so many of my other plants I bank on its help to give those stringy remains the coup de grâce.

To eradicate the tenacious taproots of dandelions, or of the self-seeded robinias and oaks, I have a tool that looks like a large screwdriver with a split tip like a snake's tongue. For vegetable beds I can recommend a Dutch hoe, which resembles

A slop sink in Emmenthal in Switzerland

a stirrup on a very long handle. It allows me to work quickly between rows without trampling the soil, provided I can get this done early in the season and do it regularly, as it cannot deal with weeds that have already become tough. Since it merely decapitates them it has to be repeated every few weeks, but in the end you will prevail. For people whose time and energy is limited, a new method was invented by a gutsy woman from Kansas, who made a miraculous discovery. This was Ruth Stout, who took up vegetable gardening in her late forties and proceeded to become the Queen of Mulch. She had migrated from Kansas to stony Connecticut, where she gardened well into her seventies and wrote down her pithy observations in a small book entitled *How to Have a Green Thumb without an Aching Back*. In it she recounts the critical moment when she suddenly noticed that a patch of soil beneath a layer of discarded vegetable scraps had remained soft and friable through the winter and was ready to be planted in spring without further ado, that is to say without turning the soil. As a freshly baked missionary she worked away at spreading her gospel as well as her compost, which like most religion was slow in latching on. Throwing away spade and hoe is not everybody's idea of gardening, but decades later—her book was published in 1970—mulching became a cornerstone of organic gardening.

Mulch can be almost any material, from dry leaves to straw, spoiled hay, shredded newspapers, spent hops, mushroom compost, pine needles, bark chips, even stones—or whatever you can lay your hands on. Salt hay for a while was considered the thing to have; it was chic and expensive, and slow in breaking down. I find small particles that decompose quickly preferable, since in doing so they add humus to the soil. Then there are sheets of plastic; they work but are unsightly and do not let the rain through. New fabrics are invented all the time, better looking and permeable. I consider them only for kitchen gardens or new beds, until the shrubs and perennials in them have become established. The benefit of applying such a top dressing is threefold. It smothers the weeds, depriving them of light and air. The few that push up anyway are weak and therefore easy to lift. Even more important is that it conserves moisture by reducing surface evaporation. If that is your primary reason for mulching, and it is mine, we have to make sure that the area in question gets thoroughly watered before we put down the mulch of our choice. Allegedly mulch also puts up a barrier that seems to keep pests and diseases at a minimum. I am not sure why, but am not one to argue with success.

One of the attractions of gardening is that not only is it a manual activity, but one where marvels can be obtained with just a handful of tools. A spade, a trowel, a good pruner are all that is needed—everything else is finesse. Not quite, since watering is just as essential as weeding and so a source of water and a hose are essential wherever we live, be this in England (more weeding) or near a desert (more watering). I started with very few utensils. Straight lines were managed without a string by laying the long handle of my rake on the ground and sprinkling the seeds alongside. I was oblivious to the existence of a dibber until I was given an antique one for my fiftieth birthday. Up to that point I had made the holes for small bulbs or young leeks by using the handle of my trowel. I am not a gadgeteer and less is more, everywhere else too, except in the bank. But when we delve deeper into the soil a wheelbarrow becomes indispensable, and suddenly we see a better pair of secateurs, consider them an improvement over the one we have, which needs sharpening anyway, and surely a pruner with long handles would make more sense too since I have more strength in two arms than in one hand. But by and large I have added only a few extras over the years: the earlier mentioned Dutch hoe for one, and a very practical, expandable metal rake. I am fully aware that I use my spade—a planting spade—the wrong way, because it is small, which is all I can handle, though turning the soil takes twice as long. At some point I sent for a fork from a catalog house, when I discovered a stainless steel one with a hollow handle. For unless an object is easy to lift, I opt against it. With advancing years the weight of everything becomes a consideration and I even take coats off the rack in shops to first see how heavy they are. Most of them go straight back. Idem umbrellas. My one indulgence are baskets of any kind. They are lighter than they look, often handsomely crafted and of impressive durability. Having come to terms with the likelihood that they will outlive me, I take special care of them every fall. I brush them and then hose them down with a sharp jet of water. When they are dry I apply a thin coat of wax, and lastly buff them with an old sock. This adds another year to their life. It is that extra year we all would like to get.

None of these tools gets obsolete, and mercifully my tools are in an old chicken house, where I am sheltered from suggestions by the maddening crowd that I really need a new computer, should buy an iPad or an iPod, a Kindle or an Android, or whatever is next on this list of new toys that turns us into victims of consumerism and cogs in the machinery of economics. There is a lot to be said for the small hand rake with its dried out wooden handle which did yeoman's duty for me during the last forty years. It was already a hand-me-down when I got it from its owner, and an era came to an end when I had to replace it recently with a brand new one, devoid of all sentimental connotations. Whatever utensils I have, they are here to stay. The Italian customs officials made fun of me when I arrived from the U.S. with my planting spade and hollow-handled fork in hand. They thought I did not know that such items could be bought in their country too. I suspect I am not the only person with such a predilection. There are few garden instruments that have survived the centuries. Made of wood and iron, they were repaired again and again. When they finally succumbed, the local blacksmith recycled the metal part and hand-forged it into a new spade or sickle or whatever, which accounts for some minor variations in design. These sometimes reveal in what region the tool originated. The tasks that they had to help execute, however, stayed the same. Major changes in gardening techniques were relatively few; until recently, agriculture was not notable for having many revolutions either, considering that we have been at it for roughly ten thousand years. True, animals were harnessed and yoked, the plough was introduced, the wheel invent-

ed, and ingenious irrigation systems devised. Horse power was provided by mules, oxen, and water buffaloes too, until the industrial revolution rolled around and engines began to take over, resulting in unprecedented changes. For the past hundred years, machines and vehicles have become steadily bigger and more impressive and are now indispensable, to the extent that the modern farmer needs to be as much of a mechanic as a plantsman. Smallholders often lack the funds to acquire a new tractor when the old one breaks down. The *agricoltori* in our Italian valley take turns in renting the gigantic *trebbia* threshing machine, a multitasking behemoth which they try to get ahold of close to the full moon so they can work through the night. And as the wheels of time turn faster and faster, we are facing a sea change of a very different nature. Genetic engineering dangles temptation in front of our nose that would let humanity take quantum leaps forward. At the same time we are filled with anxiety and skepticism, fearful that we are building an ever higher house of cards.

Horticultural tasks and tools likewise stayed put for generations, with the occasional introduction of some modest mechanization such as the old-fashioned lawnmowers. But then, suddenly, with a twentieth-century bang, a group of electric power tools—the lawnmower, the chainsaw, the rototiller, the leaf blower, the weed eater, and the electric shears—were put at our disposal. They have one thing

At Villa Gamberaia near Florence ▲

in common: they make a lot of noise and announce Saturday as clearly as church bells let us know it is Sunday. Despite the machinery of the modern age, the name of the game is still manpower. Italian craftsmen and laborers such as carpenters and plumbers, for instance, list the hours of labor on their invoices as *mano d'opera*: handiwork. And handiwork is indeed what we apply in the garden. Weeding, thinning out, planting, staking, training, cutting back, raking, and harvesting are all done manually. Even when it comes to pest control, ecologists recommended picking the little buggers by hand. I have stayed away so far from mentioning this problematic issue, which is of worrisome importance.

I fondly reminisce about the honeymoon days of gardening in Katonah, where success was paired with a lighthearted attitude. My young garden was healthy and I did not spend too much time thinking about it all. It was an out-of-sight, out-of-mind kind of involvement. Pests and diseases had not yet focused in on me. They got wind a year or two later of a garden patch where feasts could be had for the asking. They all arrived in a single season: cutworms, aphids, spittlebugs, tomato hornworms, Colorado beetles, Japanese beetles, and deer, steadily multiplying thereafter. After three years, their orgies were in full swing. For ecologically sensitive gardeners the question of whether to spray or not does not even arise. They refuse to hear about chemicals and order praying mantis eggs, pints of ladybugs, and pounds of pyrethrum, all of which gladden their hearts because they are made by nature. I tried those furry balls containing mantis eggs and suspended them in the branch of a tree as instructed by the accompanying brochure. Of course I felt gratified when I sighted a live but rather small mantis at the tail end of the summer. She was really praying, but where were the others? And had her appetite made a differ-

ence? As for the ladybugs, I could not wait to deposit the contents of the small cotton bag into the vegetable garden the moment I received them in the mail. Thirty-six hours later I found the dotted bugs in the same spot in a sad little heap. They were dead. They should have been set free only after the arrival of aphids, or they were doomed to die of starvation, which they did. The following year I carefully stored

Strawberry fields in Ireland

the cotton bag with the fresh supply in the drawer of the refrigerator, to keep them quiet as instructed, waiting for the aphids to put in their appearance. You should have heard the histrionics of Adell, our housekeeper, when she pulled her hand from the fridge, where the ladybugs had made a getaway and crawled up her arm by the hundreds. The truth is, a ladybug is a pretty creature by itself, and a solitary grasshopper in a flower is a thing of great beauty. Even stinkbugs can have their oscillating charm. But when you see them in legions, their decorative value vanishes and we recoil.

Tidying up never stops.

Reluctantly, we have to recognize that nature stacked the odds in favor of pests and diseases. There are more than five million species of insects alone, while we mammals try to muddle through with a mere five thousand, some of us endangered. And there are, must be, many insects still waiting to be discovered and classified. It was the Japanese beetles that decidedly irritated me. They were a most unfortunate import to the U.S. and are now also beginning to show up in Europe. I had read that in Japan they have a natural enemy in the form of milky spore bacteria. The agricultural extension of Dutchess County helped direct me to a husband-and-wife team of scientists who had taken it upon themselves to produce these bacteria for commercial use. They showed up, two very old people significantly arriving in a Volkswagen Beetle. Upon inspecting our little buggers they jubilated when they found a white spot on the thorax of some of them, which apparently meant they were not long for this world. The other millions were alive and kicking, and so I bought several pounds of milky spore bacteria at an alarming price. It came in the form of a white powdered substance, packed into old coffee tins. All I had to do was put down a teaspoon full of the stuff on the lawn in a grid pattern of one foot apart. As I distributed a fortune's worth of what might have been cornstarch or talcum powder, I became a bit skeptical and politely declined the offer of the old couple to put up beetle traps throughout our property in order to intensify their studies. We had enough beetles of our own without those of our neighbors. Nothing ever happened, and nothing improved. The slothful, gluttonous parasites devoured every single rosebud just like before, consumed every raspberry, and transformed yards of foliage into delicate lacework. But I need not have worried about the couple's honesty. Several years later I heard that two strains of milky spore bacteria existed. Our scientists had cultured the wrong one.

My sympathies remain with organic gardeners. However, I am not a fanatic and when faced with a real menace I cave in and occasionally resort to chemical intervention. Nobody is suggesting wholesale carpet bombing with toxic substances that have catastrophic consequences. The operative word is judicious. If a careful application of the right fungicide saves a vulnerable clematis from wilting at a galloping pace, I will use it. And rather than witnessing a transplanted three-year-old linden tree perish due to the relentless sucking of the nearly invisible red spider, or having my large-leaved evergreen bushes chewed to bits by the nightly activities of the black vine weevil, I definitely try to find the right and rapid remedy, chemical or not. Simultaneously, I have begun to harbor a sneaking suspicion that some boastful organic gardeners are like those vegetarians who eat meat when nobody is looking. The will is there, but the flesh is weak. Spraying some poisons are practices that we can let pass on a small scale; we permit them in the creation of those fantasy plots that our gardens are. In agriculture, however, they have taken on dimensions that make them utterly unacceptable.

Finally, there is another question: who is doing all the work in the garden? Most of us enthusiasts start out by wanting to master it all alone. If we have the discipline to stay small that is a distinct possibility. All we need is a patch of land and a little bit of time. But sooner or later we add this or that, a flower border, or maybe a decorative kitchen garden, and then find out that some of the maintenance requires more care, strength, and endurance than we have. We come to the conclusion that we need a lot of time and a little money too. Or, alternatively, a little time and a lot of money. And before long we up the ante and consider the possibility of hired help. But few people today can afford a full-time professional gardener, particularly one who lives in a ravishing cottage on one's property. My mother was very lucky in that respect, for when she inherited her father's house in Zurich at the age of nineteen, Herr Heidegger, the resident gardener, stayed on. He was the old-fashioned type from the upstairs–downstairs school, who was not only an expert horticulturalist but also knew all his employer's wishes before he or she had uttered them. Alas, by the time my brother and I were born, he had become a myth. The old world had changed, particularly in the realm of domestic service. During the follow-

The famous onion market in Bern takes place every November.

ing eighteen years we had a succession of three different gardeners, when previously it was a lifetime engagement. I remember Herr Bertschinger, an ill-tempered man with a very red face, suffering from high blood pressure and arthritis. So much for the notion that gardening keeps you happy, healthy, and your blood pressure low. He was replaced by Herr Ritter, of whom I remember nothing but his name. After that a Herr Diener was taken on, who was okay and quite handsome, but he and his wife bred like rabbits and he planted more and more cabbages, much to my mother's dismay. My father kept insisting that she should go over to their house and have a serious talk with them about birth control. But she was totally devoid of such inclinations, never broached the subject, and the Dieners left us when there was no more room in the house for the many children.

So here we are then, denizens of a new age, looking around for other possibilities to lighten the load of heavy garden work. In gentrified areas or suburbs there are maintenance firms and freelance teams, or we may be able to find the occasional Saturday afternoon teenager. It is a turning point in our lives as gardeners and feels a bit like sending your child to boarding school. A sense of alienation sets in when a hired hand pulls out the weeds for you, and some cherished young plants with it. All of a sudden you fill the boots of a director or supervisor, and when things don't go smoothly you turn into a diplomat learning to negotiate. If this suits you, you are on the road to becoming an armchair gardener. That was a form my late brother-in-law, William Rubin, brought to never-before-seen heights. Not given to timid approaches, he had only one tool, and that was a megaphone, through which he belted out his orders from the floriferous terrace of his house in the south of France to his gardener Alain, working on the grounds below.

◄ Counting your seeds and waiting for spring.

The Draughtsman's Contract

While climate and soil are the main factors that determine what plants we can grow, the lay of the land and the site itself have a say, too, in the making of our outdoor habitats. For what captures the visitor's attention first when stepping through the garden gate is not the details of the planting but an overall impression of architecture and style. Many frameworks have been devised over the centuries to display the greenery of our choice. Different approaches and themes exist, and we encounter every facet of past and present garden history, from faithful recreations of French parterres to a newly formulated modern wilderness. The latest additions to that list are certain conceptual designs, which we find disconcerting: rock gardens without the alpines, or Japanese inspired sculpture gardens devoid of heritage and innate tradition. They all illustrate the phases we have gone through in our domestication of nature, yet inevitably are renderings of our current yearnings, for even when we are able to create a landscape that has a timeless quality to it, it is never that but a representation of our own epoch.

No matter what esthetic we subscribe to, a proper garden needs the support of some form of construction. This is more grandly known as landscape architecture. While the principal players are plants, a plan and some foundation work are needed to show these off, to emphasize their characteristics and promote their growth. That it takes more than weeding to create a garden is born out by the etymology of the words "yard" and "garden," which allegedly go back to the old English *geard*, meaning wattle fence. Wattle formed the first boundaries for a favored plot of earth. It cannot have taken very long to replace it with something more solid to define the enclosure that came to be named the garden. Wattle, or wicker fencing, formerly crafted on site where needed, has become a portable item these days, sold in prefabricated sections of various dimension at fashionable flower fairs. The stands that offer them are not far from those of nurseries peddling their mints, comfreys, and bible

◄ A couple takes a stroll on the cypress walk at
Giardino Giusti in Verona. Romeo and Juliet perhaps?

leaf, full of lore and old wives' tales, which are an amusing appendix of the chatty world of herbalists and minor plant collectors. Herb gardens, along with their classic companion, wattle, connect us to an early form of horticulture, the European archetype of which was an enclosure of geometric little beds, each contained and filled with aromatic plants. Originally found in the courtyard of monasteries, the herb garden served a utilitarian purpose and was called the physic garden, which was the virtual ancestor of our pharmacy.

This authentic twelfth-century monastery courtyard from southern France found its final station at The Cloisters in New York City.

A delightful feature at Certosa di Pavia, a splendid Carthusian charterhouse in Lombardy built during the fourteenth century, is the nuns' quarters, where each cell opens up to a very small, walled-in *hortus conclusus* of its own. These are now bare, with a little stone seat here or an empty flower bed there, full of suggestive powers that bring your mind instantly to the question of which plants you would select if this were your own playground. There is a lot to be said for such a small garden, and it is a tempting exercise to decide which four or five plants would be your "must haves" were you confined to such a small area. For me, it would be *Abutilon megapotamicum*, and then of course I would have to have an intensely fragrant rose with a protracted flowering season, producing beautiful hips (I'd better give this some study first), and also three hostas with huge leaves in the sheltered corner, where they cannot get ripped to shreds by a hailstorm early in the season. I'd sneak in some bronze-colored miniature tulips battalini underneath. I think I would need a pearl bush too. And a perovskia. And of course some yellow raspberries. We'll see. It is a happy and frequently changing fantasy, without the intimidating weight of a huge

A private walled garden in Granada, Spain

garden with hundreds of plants and too many options. Options—a glib word. Perfect for those suave youngsters who confuse members of my generation when explaining some functions on our electronic instruments. In my opinion, fewer choices are an advantage: too many options spoil the broth. Luckily, the history of garden architecture gives us some relief in that respect, as it simplifies everything by operating with straightforward alternatives. A garden can only be enclosed or open. The terrain is either hilly or flat. The style formal or informal. If you are wealthy enough, you can have all of the above, combined. That brings us to a most important question, which is how big a garden can we manage. For a garden that is too demanding and gets out of hand puts us back to the nightmare of schooldays when we had not done the homework. It is a rather unpleasant feeling. No amount of money can fix it as the laborer is hard to find. Many freelance gardeners are overburdened themselves and "under the weather": unreliable and capricious. So my advice is to accept your limits and stay small. Better to maintain and perfect.

Whether open or enclosed, big or small, gardens usually have a basic plan which, in classical design, is organized around a central axis. This straight line emphasizes the principal view and connects two chosen vantage points. The Tuscan nobleman, for instance, could look from the piano nobile of his palazzo to the terrace below, which presented him with an elegantly patterned parterre of soothing symmetry and pleasing size, leading his eye through an opening in the enclosing hedge to the rolling hills beyond. Catherine de Medici undoubtedly took that main axis along with her to France, where it eventually enabled the great Louis XIV to gaze from his bedroom over a controlled scene of stone, earth, and water, as far as the eye could see. He felt reassured by its rigid geometry and comforted by the splendid subjugation of nature. An axis, created by man and never by nature, can be anything: a canal, an allée of trees, a straight riding path through the woods, or a double perennial border backed by fat yew hedges. In large gardens this main coordinate is sometimes placed independently of the house, with "green rooms" going off to one or both sides, a nod to the original *giardino secreto* of the Italian Renaissance, where a smaller and separate enclosure was concealed from the main view. This idea of green rooms has become an important theme in many of the great gardens that have been created since then.

Reaching back to the eighteenth century we find a fundamental change that took place. It was the English who began to look at their surroundings with enlightened eyes and sensed that nature did not need to be despotically dominated. Under the aegis of the designers Bridgeman, Kent, Brown, and co. a much looser style of landscaping was introduced. Asymmetry gained ascendancy and the concept of a

This beautiful old Swiss farmhouse in the canton of Bern is complemented by a neatly kept vegetable garden in front of it and does its owner proud.

harmonious balance became the new ideal. The formal tradition of centuries was thrown out the window, and with it often the gardens themselves. Human involvement that expressed itself in straight lines and right angles was suddenly undesirable, while curving hills, winding paths, meandering streams, groves, and dells became the sought-after fashion of the day. Before long, pretty ruins and small temples dotted these serpentine landscapes. Bucolic idylls and Virgilian scenes bounced back at the viewer via the paintings of Poussin and Le Lorrain. Symmetry was decidedly out, though the formal side of garden art never disappeared totally. Truly new ideas appear rarely, but certainly did in England when its landskip movement took off. It found a sequel in our contemporary world, where a naturalized look is embraced by many enthusiasts who pursue a similar philosophy of freedom and reject the visible constraints imposed by landscape architecture.

The secret garden at ►►
Palazzina Farnese in Caprarola

An interlude of formality was brought into play again in the nineteenth century, when tropical flowers and ornamental plants received increased attention and wealthy country house owners felt compelled to display these imported, exotic treasures in overtly ostentatious surroundings. Enter Gertrude Jekyll, who was working at her pictorial gardens and painterly color schemes, leading the taste away from the conspicuous consumption of rigid carpet bedding toward a more relaxed style. She loved to drape honeysuckles and rambling roses over pergolas and welcomed the invasion of frothy plants that sprang up in cracks and crevices, spilling over masonry. Blurring the hard lines of architecture became her distinct signature, though her designs rested on fairly formal principles that required extensive installations. It took another century to define a more casual version of informality, yet her taste has kept a hold over our imagination. Equal credit for lasting impact must be given to a similarly gifted man. No, not Lutjens, but William Robinson of *Wild Garden* fame, whose enthusiasm for indigenous plants and native habitats along with his journalistic activities gained him a wide audience, ready to accept a completely new and ultimately more practical approach to gardening. Jekyll and Robinson would be immensely pleased if they could meander through the parks of Paris today, where the stodgy municipal flower beds of old have been refurbished under an Anglo-Saxon influence, which we often call, not entirely correctly, romantic or natural. Both Jekyll and Robinson, incidentally, were excellent writers and knew exactly what they wanted to say.

All these aforementioned styles live on side by side and inform our choices wherever a garden is made. The topography itself is likely to suggest what treatment would work best. Patterned layouts, parterres, knot gardens, mazes, and carpet bed-

From left to right:

The parterre of Villa Torrigiani near Lucca in Tuscany is waiting to be planted.

The formal terrace at Villa Tössertobel in Winterthur, Switzerland, situated next to a steep drop off in the terrain, has a main axis that connects the mansion with the solarium at the end of the garden.

A roof terrace at Le Celle Hermitage near Cortona in Italy

ding lend themselves to dealing with flat land. Hilly terrain, on the other hand, is a different story as it carries with it a much wider range of possibilities. I am not fond of flat terrain. To make an interesting garden from scratch is never easy, but to be faced with a large, open space is particularly challenging as it does not even give us the benefit of a starting point. It takes inventiveness and patience to come up with a good plan and then bring it to maturity. Hedges are almost indispensable, either as windbreaks or to divide the space into separate areas. In terms of upkeep, flat land has the potential danger of poor drainage—a nearly incurable condition.

And yet two of the most enchanting gardens I know are on such terrain: Villandry in France and Sissinghurst in England. They are hugely popular and influenced many garden makers of the twentieth century, although they are both extremely labor intensive, to say the least. The terrain surrounding Chateau de Villandry is not quite as hopelessly flat as Versailles or Sissinghurst. Its restoration was tackled in 1906 by Dr. Joachim Carvallo, doctor and scientist, who had bought the property and with admirable

A parterre handled differently at Agra Fort in Rajasthan.

The most enchanting parterre at Chateau de Villandry
is planted with colorful vegetables mixed with flowers.

care revived the remainders of the sixteenth-century garden which are adjacent to the chateau and occupy three different terraces. The uppermost contains a body of water, serving as a mirror and a reservoir. A small flight of steps down we find the formal parterre, which illustrates the theme of love, expressed in box-edged beds that have the shapes of broken hearts for passion, fans for flirtation, and sabers for jealousy. While your mind lingers with delight on this anecdotic handling of a classical feature, the real thrill is yet awaiting us, for another few steps further down, on the third terrace, we enter a free and sparkling rendition of a Renaissance garden that is dazzlingly planted with vegetables brought into play for their decorative value. In this apotheosis of the potager, composed of nine large squares, each subdivided into smaller geometric beds, we perceive red Swiss chard, bronze fennel, bright green lettuces, and purple cabbages with new eyes, noting their interesting textures and vivid colors. In some places they are mixed with flowers and punctuated by small rose trees, while trellised alcoves containing seats are positioned at the intersections of the squares to prevent the plan from being too one-dimensional. Mme. Marguerite Carvallo, the late wife of Dr. Car-

vallo's grandson Robert, took on the planning of the rotating crops for the dozens and dozens of small beds afresh twice a year—not an easy task, but splendidly executed. What Villandry stands out for is that it liberated many visitors from being stuck in the rut of dull traditions and clichés, inspiring them to try something new. Rosemary Verey, for one, managed a lovely scaled-down version of that grandest of kitchen gardens at Barnsley House, regaling us with new effects and amusing techniques, growing pumpkins on pergolas, planting purple beans next to lettuces splashed with pink blotches, and other such surprises, demonstrating what a versatile pastime vegetable gardening can be.

Sissinghurst's attraction and popularity, on the other hand, is to be attributed not only to its highbrow connection with the Bloomsbury group but also to the bird's-eye view of the garden from its tower, from where the clever plan can be clearly seen and studied. Add to this that each room or area when seen close up has a brilliantly carried out theme, such as a white garden, the rose garden, the green rondel, the nuttery, and so forth. In their heyday these enclosures were richly fur-

From the tower at Sissinghurst in Kent we can clearly see the elaborate plan of the green rooms.

nished with a multitude of flowers, about which Vita Sackville-West wrote in her garden column for *The Observer*. Many gardeners love to write, or at least make lists, which allows them to carry over their horticultural passion to the bleaker seasons or hours when digging, planting, and clipping is not on. Green fingers have an urge to wield...a pen!

Creating a garden on a hillside requires imagination too, albeit of a different kind. Gazing at undulating terrain, at hills and mounds and ravines, sets our mind in motion. As we trace the configuration of the surface with our eyes, we start carpeting the softly rolling land with flowering meadows and dot them with fruit trees, then embellish the crest of a hillock with a group of shrubs, or artfully tuck away a body of water behind a mound, hidden from the main view, so as to chance upon it by surprise. A lot depends on the incline of the land. Where it is steep, practical considerations take precedence over fantasy: we have no choice but must level parts of it if something other than grass is to grow. Soil erosion has to be kept in bounds or else we will see precious earth dribble downhill the moment we put a spade into the ground. Nor must the water be allowed to run away too fast either. Terracing is the time-honored way to deal with this problem. Whether for better or for worse, it changes the contours of the land, as we sometimes notice when driving past abandoned vineyards, where the carved tiers remain visible long after viniculture stopped. Where farming goes on at steep mountain sides, the sight is truly spellbinding. I am thinking of the rice terraces in Asia, which are striking testimonies to human toil and endurance and nourish billions of people. Or of the fabulous lemon groves on the Amalfi coast. A more recent invention is the technique of contour farming, in which horizontal bands of different crops are planted on sloping land, so that the cultivation of each crop—alfalfa alternating with corn, for instance—takes place at a different time and thus prevents the loss of soil which would be inevitable were heavy machinery brought in to do the tilling and harvesting of a whole hillside all at the same time. Not only does contour or strip farming keep unwanted monocultures away but it also presents us with a handsomely patterned landscape.

Dumbarton Oaks in Washington D.C. is considered one of the best hillside gardens in the U.S. Its large grounds were bought by Mr. and Mrs. Robert Bliss in 1920 when, after years in diplomatic service and its extensive travels, they were ready to settle down and find the right premises for their collection of Byzantine and Pre-Columbian art. A Federalist house and a farm originally named The Oaks made the property the perfect place for them. But even more important than the purchase was their choice of Beatrix Farrand, the successful garden designer whose early cultural and architectural education had been taken in hand by her garden-loving aunt, the writer Edith Wharton. Luckily, Beatrix Farrand accepted the offered commission, which blossomed into an involvement and teamwork that lasted twenty-six years. In a felicitous partnership, Mildred Bliss and Beatrix Farrand—both very cultured ladies—dedicated themselves to the remodeling of this rugged hill, while Mr. Robert Wood Bliss, still active as a diplomat, set the tone for the outdoor areas destined for their happy family life. Social gatherings of a more official nature also were catered to. The so-called Green Garden not far from the mansion was purposely designed as a simple background to better show off the cocktail dresses of the lady guests.

The actual genius of the place is its hillside location; it predestined Dumbarton Oaks to hark back to Italian Renaissance gardens. No coincidence this: popes and dukes purposely established their summer residences in the hills near Rome or Florence as these offered refreshing breezes during the hot season. This link may well be what attracted the Blisses when they acquired this difficult site, which other people might not have considered. For a start, extensive masonry work was carried out to create myriad different enclosures, terraces, a rose garden, swimming pool and tennis court, and other theme gardens that sprawl downward toward the more naturalized areas abutting Rock Creek. Classical plants like yew, holly, and boxwood were made lavish use of to add a good part of the green bones. Most of these outdoor sections, whether grand or intimate, have a certain European flair and are embellished with ornaments in the best of taste. Balustrades, urns, fountains, vases, sculptures, mosaics, and furniture abound and were designed for their precise location, frequently by Beatrix Farrand herself. The quality of craftsmanship throughout is such that we can still enjoy this amazing garden a hundred years after its creation. Dumbarton Oaks is exceptional inasmuch as it is not a copy or mere imitation of an Italian garden. The absence of a strictly formal and symmetric plan alone tells us that it was not conceived on the drawing board and then forcefully imposed on the grounds. Beatrix Farrand was guided by what was in front of her eyes. She had the good sense to preserve many of the existing specimen trees and integrate them into the overall design. Over the course of the long collaboration, more than twenty-five specific sites were created, pleasantly adapted to the lay of the land. Each descent to another level received a suitable treatment. Formal stone stairs, grassed steps, curving brick paths, and simple descents bring the visitor to another area. Formality dissolves in the region way down towards the creek, where Crabapple Hill, Forsythia Dell, and Lovers Lane Pond were developed. Surprise is the strong suit of this romantic garden and gives it its unique character and twentieth-century feeling. Meandering around, we get lost in our dreamy thoughts and in the garden itself: without a map in our hand we would not find the exit very rapidly, nor would we want to.

The majority of gardens, however, are not as grand as the examples described above, but they too benefit from a plan or a clear idea. The ideal case would be the one where we buy or rent a house because we really fell in love with its garden. This can happen, but usually it's the other way around and we choose the house first and foremost, regarding the backyard as a secondary issue to which we may or may not want to make some changes later on. Whatever we plan to do to it, an existing garden is definitely easier to handle than a stark empty yard because its live furnishings provide scale and perspective, which will give us a head start, even when we do not

At Dumbarton Oaks, the long Box Walk descends softly to a focal point, the Ellipse.

Two concentric ellipses formed by hornbeam trees surround
a lawn adorned by an antique Provençal fountain at its center.

An old *pineta* and a small garden house is what we see from a first-floor window at Contessa Giuppi Pietromarchi's Tuscan villa in Capalbio, Italy.

approve of its contents as such. You live with your view for a while, find that the hedge in the back may not be all that bad, and all of a sudden are tempted to apply a few nips and tucks here, plant some roses there, eventually decide on an altogether different look and select the big, fat, dark red rhododendron in the middle as a specimen for euthanasia so that you can plant an apple tree—slightly off center—instead. Let me assure you that the rhododendron will come out of this scenario alive, for some friendly neighbor will consent to transplant it to her own garden, or a nurseryman will take it off your hands and profitably sell it on as a valuable mature item.

Small gardens are easier to handle, and the owners oftentimes want to have a go at it themselves rather than involve a professional designer. Where bigger acreage is concerned the story is a different one. The question is less whether to engage a landscape architect than to find the right one. A good garden designer is able to carve a piece of open land and render it more intimate, or achieve the opposite and make a small plot look bigger. Steering the clients towards formality or suggesting a

From an adjacent window we are offered a parallel view: Giuppi standing in the doorway of her studio at the lower end of the garden, seemingly perched in the window of the gazebo. Real, not Photoshopped.

more casual look is also what he or she must do at the outset. Interviewing husband and wife together when proposing a design is a smart idea to make sure that they are in agreement, because radical changes in the garden are known to cause heated arguments, even among otherwise peaceful couples, who suddenly begin to battle with each other as if they were on opposite sides in a civil war.

I knew and am friends with a number of garden designers, but none as exotic and imposing as Russell Page, who was a giant in his field. R.P. was already quite old when I met him, and seemingly lonely, though one could not be quite sure of that as he was discreet beyond measure. Sometimes he worked nearby for weeks without giving a sign of life, and then just when I thought that he was going to stay in our neck of the woods for a while, it turned out that he was literally on his way to the airport to fly off to South America or back to England. I think he cultivated this aspect of mysterious departures and arrivals. He was not what you would call an open book. In his youth he had fallen under the spell of the mystic Gurdjieff, an exposure that left its distinct mark as he married Gurdjieff's daughter.

Stairway to heaven: the painter Jennifer Bartlett's roof garden
on top of her house in Charles Street, Manhattan, New York.

Not mysticism but a love of plants had created a spontaneous friendship between us. Most gardeners exude some kind of theoretical sympathy for each other,
a bit like Freemasons must have had between them in the past, or so I imagine. We
had in common that we worked for clients, rendering a service. I was amazed when
I heard how Page ran his business, which is to say not at all. When I suggested he
might consider taking an agent or a representative, he responded that what he really needed was a nanny. Despite the absence of the latter, he was always handsomely
dressed in old corduroy jackets or blazers, and was as well-groomed as befits a British gentleman. When I told him I had just heard that human hair purportedly was
a viable deer repellent, he laughed loud, touched the top of his bald head and said
he was sorry to have so little to offer in that respect. Later he got up and asked for

Stairs humanize a garden
and exist in many styles.

Clockwise from top:

Palazzo Brandolini in Venice

La Mortella, Ischia

Dumbarton Oaks, Washington D.C.

Parc de St. Cloud, Paris

Villa Gamberaia, near Florence

the facilities so that he could wash his "paws." These paws were actually fairly large, sensitive hands that had immediately caught my attention at our first encounter when I took his portrait in his apartment at Cadogan Gardens in London. As my gaze was fixed upon them he suddenly brought up Oskar Kokoschka's early paintings as if he had been reading my mind. I thought it rather uncanny until I found out that he had studied under Kokoschka in his youth.

Page's conversation was peppered with marquesses and duchesses, barons and dukes, but in all fairness it must be said that this probably had more to do with the kind of clientele that requested formal gardens than with name dropping in order to impress. On the whole, however, I imagined that he would have been happier living in another century, working for some nobleman, being granted privileges and given lodgings in a separate part of the chateau. He once told me he felt his clients should pay him what his work seemed worth to them. This put some garden owners into such a quandary that as a result no money changed hands. My understanding of his professional life grew when I undertook the task of photographing his gardens, or maybe I should say what was left of them. I was usually put up at the owners' house so as to catch the earliest morning light and much enjoyed this convenience. The hosts were often charming and the atmosphere in general reflected the congenial relationship Page had with his clients. He chose them as much as they had chosen him. He also loved being looked after, free to concentrate on plans and plants. Whenever I invited him for dinner in Katonah I made sure the meals were of quality, assuming that he was partial to the pleasures of the table. I once prepared a pasta primavera on such an occasion for which my photographer friend Elisabeth Novick helped me peel every single pea one by one as the American peas were too big to qualify as fine food. Another time, when I was fairly sure he would not suddenly vanish to another continent, I made an ice-cream sculpture of a flower basket that took me three days to assemble. I think he liked being coddled in that way. What he hated most was to run the risk of being asked to visit the gardens of neighboring ladies who vied for his attention like schoolgirls and expected to be given grades for their horticultural abilities. They would have been better off shelling peas.

Russell P. threw his net wide, conscious of the landscape as a whole, the sky above and the mud below, with that layer of earth in between, where a particular kind of garden magic might be coaxed into existence. More than paths and hedges were necessary to catch that elusive quality he aspired to. His aim was to prepare the stage on which nature would perform her best play. Or, in other circumstances, he would shoot for a place of chaste, uncluttered beauty, inviting solitude and meditation. Whatever his goal, many factors had to be taken into account to attain the desired result. To start with, a quintessential sense of proportion was needed to establish scale, order, and coherence. The varying characteristics of light and shade had to be considered, and the distribution of volumes studied. Not to speak of the imponderables and complexities of the negative spaces in between. Next in line was the planning of the green architecture and the choreography of seasonal botanical happenings. For Page there was a deeper meaning to it all. But in all his strivings for that greater perfection he never lost sight of the fact that gardening is a craft, based on practical knowhow and a knowledge of plants. Even if he had his occasional flirts with the high-maintenance parks of the past, as a designer he was fully aware that his clients lived in the modern age, where the availability of labor was restricted and the budget often limited. If knot gardens and parterres had to be designed, he kept them simple and elegant. He was enamored of water and introduced it whenever he could, making sure it could be done without problems. Page was also an excellent teacher, opening people's eyes to plant form and leaf texture and how these could and should be brought into the larger composition. Acutely aware of the perishability of gardens he had designed, he wrote a book about his craft in a lucid and distinguished style. It made him famous beyond his fieldwork, as the many gardens he had designed were in private hands and had never been seen by the public at large. Thus his book *The Education of a Gardener* became his most permanent achievement.

Russell Page at his London apartment in 1980

Leaves of Grass
and Bales of Hay

Despite their singularly unimpressive flowers I have a particular fondness for grasses. The *Gramineae* are a very large family of about ten thousand sub-species and, counted individual by individual, they possibly outnumber those of all other plants combined. They have been around for millions of years and ingratiated themselves to us from the start, even before our Neolithic ancestors had the idea to put two and two together and plant their seeds. Some grasses give us the staff of life, while others provide carpeting for our outdoor habitats, and sometimes for the roofs over our heads as well. They dominate large natural areas called prairies, steppes, and savannas, and constitute an overwhelming portion of our farmland. In Switzerland, where I grew up, grass was everywhere, in the lowlands and the Alps, in stables and haylofts, on golf courses and on schoolroom walls, where our drawings of grasses and meadow flowers got pinned up as temporary exhibits. My bedroom at home, on the other hand, was adorned with a framed reproduction of one of the great masterpieces of art, Albrecht Dürer's *Das große Rasenstück* (The Large Piece of Turf). Its title alone has majestic weight. It is fascinating to see with how many weeds Albrecht Dürer endowed that gorgeous piece of turf. In between the grasses we find budding dandelion, the leaves of plantains, veronicas, pimpinellas, achilleas, and daisies, all given equal play and lovingly depicted with that northern love of detail combined with the sensuous brushstroke Dürer had acquired in Italy. Several of these subjects are excellent forage for animals, yet at the same time are awaited with bells on by the chemical industry, which targets them as enemies to be eliminated at all cost the minute they dare to appear in your lawn.

My favorite part of our large garden in Zurich was just such a meadow of mixed grasses mingling with a multitude of humble flowers. Its care was entrusted to a neighboring farmer, who came to cut the grass with a scythe in late spring or early summer—always too soon for me. I still prefer to see mowing in the Alps done at the last

◄ Six-foot-high *Miscanthus sinensis* "Gracillimus" near a swimming pool looks fabulous even in winter.

possible moment, though it may be better husbandry to do it before the flowers are in full bloom. Later in summer the farmer would bring around his cows to graze, for free of course, in exchange for the opulent cow pads they left behind. This was a barter that filled me with deep skepticism, but now that manure is so hard to find I see it as a real bargain. If the upkeep of meadows were without hitches we would probably see more of them, as they fill the distinct role of satisfying our current preference for a type of landscape that lies somewhere between the wilderness and an overly manicured garden.

What is undisputed, however, is that the star performers among the *Gramineae* are our main food plants: wheat, rice, corn, barley, oats, and rye. Wheat is the world's preeminent grain with the longest running show. It shaped our history, our landscapes, our wealth. An ear of wheat is an emblem of fertility that conjures up its impressive curriculum like a memory card. It rose to the top very early on for something more than its nutritional value: it is storable and transportable. These attributes gave it a clear advantage in the days of gathering food from the wild by bridging the gaps caused by history's recurrent food shortages. Its flour lends itself to being formed into biscuits and bread that can be given distinct shape, especially when leavened. It raised the developing society above the lowest culinary level of eating amorphous porridges and pulses, and it is easy to understand that bread thus attained ceremonial or sacred status. Enterprising men and women of the Iron Age paid great attention to this grass, selecting the ones with the largest and plumpest grains they could find, first in the wild, and then among those they were cultivating. Other factors were taken notice of also, for instance that some types of wheat grains did not shatter as easily as others. The botanical term for this characteristic is "indehiscent," an important feature that eliminated the laborious task of gleaning single seeds from the ground. Bringing sheaves of wheat intact to a threshing place was a step forward, and we can claim that agriculture and botany took off simultaneously roughly 10,000 years ago. The pretty ear of wheat as we know it has undergone a steady stream of developments since then, culminating in those of the Green Revolution in the middle of the twentieth century, when deliberate crossbreeding of wheat with rye led to a new hybrid named triticale, which yielded hitherto unknown bumper crops. But the resulting hubris was soon dampened by the anticlimactic realization that we were becoming totally dependent on fertilizers and irrigation, herbicides, pesticides, fungicides, and heavy machinery. It also came at a high ecological cost, because many of the less productive varieties of wheat were left behind and drifted towards the brink of extinction. Let us hope that this deceptive triumph will remain a warning example for people of the twenty-first century, alerting us to the dangers that may be hidden in the new breeding techniques, tissue culture, irradiation, chromosome doubling, and whatever else the meddling with genetics will bring.

A field of farro ▶

Other grains suitable for growing on poorer soils, or where the climate is too cold or wet to grow wheat, are rye, barley, and oats. They all have merits beyond supplying us with sustenance. Rye, for instance, sometimes grows to two meters tall and produces stalks much in demand for the stalls of pampered racehorses, or for making straw hats and other woven objects. And indeed, where would we be without that Italian straw hat—on screen and off. But more importantly to some of my friends, the winter-hardy rye is also used for brewing beer and spirits. It seems that tippling is right up there among the basic human needs along with food, sex, and shelter, for there is hardly a variety of grain that has not been tried for making booze. Once brewing whiskey latched on in northern Europe, barley began to have mass appeal. Up to that point it had only been used as food; in classical Rome, bread was made from barley flour because wheat was too expensive for the populace at large. Ceres, the Roman goddess of agriculture, wears a wreath of barley on her head, and her name is honored in our daily use of the word cereal. Of all the grains mentioned, only oats are free of alcoholic association. They are fit to grow in the wettest of climates and are considered wholesomeness itself for many parts of our bodies from skin to guts. Stomach problems can be treated with oatmeal soup, while itchy skin is relieved by ablutions of milky oat bran suds. And what really should

This horse is feeling its oats.

have been mentioned first is that the velocity with which we progressed through history is in huge part due to horses, who thrived on vast amounts of that grain.

Food and drink aside, it is the looks of these grasses that please me. I love the changing hues and textures they take on during their short cycle of life. They all begin with that promising silky green and then proceed to different colors and various states of bristliness. Rye reveals itself by its bluish-gray cast, wheat by turning beige before going on to richer and richer shades of gold. Acres of ripening oats stand out by a saturated dull brown, adding yet another tint to the patchwork of fields: my favorite landscape. It is a borrowed view and a magnificent, gradually changing spectacle, accompanied by a certain melancholy since the opulent softness of the maturing crops soon will come to an end and make way for the barren look of a moonscape. Farmers are sometimes called our planet's gardeners, offering us a cultivated landscape that has a reassuring quality to it. The more old-fashioned the farmer is, the more varied the fields are, for crop rotation is the trademark of the smallholder and the sine qua non of sound farming. Too much of it has disappeared already, forcing my generation to witness massive changes, not just from spreading urbanism and ever bigger waves of cement but more insidiously from mega monocultures and reckless, market-driven agribusiness with its accompanying loss of genetic resources and the inherent possibility of disaster.

The rice culture of Asia is the one I encountered last. I was smitten by it instantly. On account of its being grown in water, which adds that wonderful extra, it is very picturesque. There exist more than fifty varieties of rice, of which ten percent grow on dry land and are sowed and harvested just like our wheat or barley. Rice is the world's leading tropical crop and shapes the lives of millions of people around the world from dawn to dusk. It is at all times a tough undertaking, and more so in mountainous regions, as hillsides have to be terraced, low walls of mud built, water has to be redirected and paddies maintained, seedlings transplanted, and harvests managed. In many regions this is done by hand and the human presence is almost always manifest. In low-lying tropical areas, where two or even three harvests can be crammed into one year, work goes on practically nonstop. When watching the

Planting rice seedlings in Thailand. ▲

Rice culture in Tonkin

Rice terraces in the mountains in Yunnan, China, at various stages of growth

workers' graceful, coordinated movements I get worried what will happen to them should their work be taken over some day by machines. How does one make it up to people who had their purpose stolen?

There is another grass inextricably intertwined with the Far East: bamboo. If ever there existed a superpower among plants, bamboo with its more than 1,400 species fits that denomination. There is no sector in Asian life where it does not have an essential role, from everyday utensils, chopsticks, water ladles, cups, fishing poles, musical instruments, to walls, trellises, mats, thatch, pips, ropes, fibers, papers, acupuncture needles, and scaffolding. Not to mention it as a source of food for giant pandas, who eat almost exclusively bamboo, twenty-five to thirty pounds a day! Chinese and Japanese art and poetry are unthinkable without it, and had Jean de La Fontaine known of its existence, he would have composed a charming fable about its steely strength, flexibility, and lightweight elegance.

This much said, I am surprised bamboo is still counted as a grass. Botanists are prone to changing the names and categories of plants, and keep switching their memberships all the time, so why not also that of bamboo? Or am I misinformed and the debate is already underway? The reclassification of plants exasperates many people when they have finally mastered the Latin names of what they grow. True, vernacular names of weeds and flowers are a delightful extension of local folklore, but the Latin nomenclature is an absolute must when we communicate with friends or professionals abroad. Calling it bamboo is not enough—we have to make a clear distinction between, let's say, *Phyllostachys viridiglaucescens* and *Semiarundinaria fastuosa*. Even the Latin names of less far-fetched plants have the tendency to get stuck at the tip of our tongues when we find ourselves in other gardens than our own. Suddenly a lot of stuttering and bowdlerizing goes on, while at home *Cimicifuga racemosa* and *Ampelopsis brevipedunculata variegata* passes my lips without a moment's hesitation. This makes me suspect that there is a tight connection between memory and precise location, for I remember clearly that I was in the bathtub in Zurich when JFK was assassinated, or in a yellow cab driving east on a cross street in Manhattan when the spacecraft Challenger exploded. Idem did I register being on Hammacher Schlemmer's second floor at the moment Gorby and the Gipper drove by. And when, on occasion, I find myself in the pantry, having a blank as to what I came to look for, all I have to do is return to the spot where the idea first hit me, and it comes back to me in a flash. Maybe the scientific basis or formula for this phenomenon and similar thought-waves like telepathy will be discovered before long, just as it was for electricity. Computer science and navigation certainly point in that direction. But I am straying far from my subject of *Bambuseae*, almost as far as some of their running roots.

There are two types of bamboo. There is the clump forming (sympodial) type, and the one that forms long roots (monopodial). If anyone should want to have them in their garden, the root system of the latter has to be kept contained with impenetrable, underground barriers half a meter deep and made of metal or cement. I am unlikely to plant bamboo, not because of its aggressive vigor but on account of its Far East connotation. Like pampas grass, yucca, monkey puzzle tree, it all too often looks jarringly out of place and I have added it to my index of inadmissibles. Bamboo is seldom well planted in Europe and I can think of only one exception. It was the Italian publisher Franco Maria Ricci, a man of exquisite taste, who most originally had a labyrinth of bamboo planted. It works out brilliantly because once you are in it you see nothing else and might as well be in China.

One of bamboo's main attractions is that it grows phenomenally fast and thus ranks high as a renewable resource. Some of the culms aspire to be trees. *Phyllostachys bambusoides*, for instance, can become twenty meters high in just a few months without—lucky them—increasing their girth with age. Their continued activity takes place underground, in their subterranean rhizomes. They have the bizarre habit—and this

Phyllostachys bambusoides, Japanese timber bamboo

they have in common with some palm trees—of blooming only once, some at the end of their lives, and then dying. Their blossoming is their swan song. This attribute drives botanists up the wall for it renders identification next to useless, if it can be caught at all, since some of them don't bloom before they are 80 to 120 years old.

A plant that resembles bamboo and also migrated from east to west is sugar cane, *Saccharum officinarum*. Its garden adaptability is zilch. It is a tropical crop and a crop only, for its looks are hopelessly unkempt. It is unique inasmuch as it stands out for provoking the extremes of emotion. As an edible substance it produces the sweetest of pleasures, but when considered in its social context can only elicit horror. For the importation of this promising plant to the West Indies gave rise to the slave trade, without which it could not have been commercialized: the whitest of substances that caused the darkest of stains in human history, for which we still have not sufficiently atoned. Sugar had arrived in the Caribbean in the cargo of Christopher Columbus, who opened the doors for a two-way exchange of plants, bringing many new vegetables back to Europe. Corn, or maize, was among them. Sugar today is rivaled by corn, which has undergone amazing hybridizations. Turned into corn syrup, it is found in all sorts of prepared foods, pushing both cane and beet sugars aside. It is one of the "big three," feeding billions of people and animals, and grows on every continent, both in temperate and subtropical zones. Small wonder that it has become the pet subject of biotechnology, which spruced up its protein, making it more nourishing. It also is the source of a surprising number of products other than food, namely adhesives, varnishes, paper, and cosmetics.

And indeed, *Zea mays*, or corn, is a plant with some exceptional characteristics, as it does not self-seed but is dependent on humans to do that job for it. Probably the same Native American who showed the immigrant settler how to bury two kernels of corn accompanied by a shrimp as fertilizer also pointed out to him that notwithstanding its strong growth, each stalk bears only one or maximum two ears of corn. Despite this, and even though it is a greedy feeder, it is the only one of the hitherto mentioned grains that has snuck into a corner of my garden. It was pure nostalgia

Sugar cane has been cultivated in Egypt for thousands of years.

A rural dwelling at Skansen, the open-air museum in Stockholm, Sweden

that made us sow a small packet of sweet American corn almost immediately after our arrival in Italy. It was a total fiasco, from our point of view at least: Our 2 by 2-meter corn patch was ransacked one night by wild boars, who gorged themselves on this sweet delicacy and quenched their thirst in the swimming pool, and then relieved themselves on the terrace nearby. So that was the end of Silver Queen.

All this time I have been circling what is a central theme, and that is the lawn. It is decidedly a controversial issue. Millions of houses have some kind of green carpet, and for a large number of people the garden is altogether synonymous with a lawn. In America there are at least 50,000 square miles of the stuff. Even modest dwellings are sometimes surrounded by it without as much as a tree or a bush—which would only present an obstacle to the lawnmower anyway... The promise of this green option makes commuting tolerable and suburban living desirable as it provides the recreational space that for many families is a must. When I first beheld the beautiful residential areas in Washington, D.C., and Westchester, New York, I was most favorably impressed by the idea of a landscape privately owned but visually enjoyed by everybody, lawn bordering on lawn without much of a division in between. Now that was democracy. Beauty for all. Where the undulating greensward was shaded by an-

A small meadow in Switzerland

cient trees it made me dream of classical landscapes and Elysian Fields, with Orpheus leading Eurydice out of hell. This fantasy lasted six days. On the seventh the worm turned. Saturday arrived and Orpheus's lyre was nowhere, nor was Pan's flute. Rattling machinery and macho mutterings took over the soundtrack, leaving me with the impression that lawnmowers run largely on testosterone, until a generation later women joined the workforce and blurred the lines between sexist tasks. When I read in Michael Pollan's *Second Nature* that suburban communities existed in the States where a house owner could get fined for not keeping his lawn cut, I concluded that a different language ruled here than what I had imagined, a new kind of tyranny that deprived its citizens of choice. Lawn and order. Surely, freedom of speech begins in the front yard. If this was not so, it was back to European gardens, separated by firm walls and dense hedges, within which everybody can do and plant exactly as they please.

But what leaves me most perplexed about the lawn, which we have come to regard as an entitlement of sorts, is that it is in fact a perverse form of gardening. A lawn is a monoculture condemned to live under the totalitarian dictatorship of men and turf managers, who spurn the leaves of grass into green uniformity by beheading them constantly, thus preventing them from ever reaching maturity or dabbling in sex; they are forced to multiply by stolons underground. No other form of plant life is tolerated, and no effort is shunned to eliminate dissidents. Even useful or pretty ones like clover and violets are forbidden. If you are the emperor of Japan it is easy to deal with them: you can have every single one carefully eliminated by weeder-women with tweezers. I have seen it with my own eyes.

The green turf was already praised in Tudor England and has come a long way. A decisive step toward progress, if that is what we want to call it, was made in 1830, when an engineer by the name of E. Budding, who lived in Gloucestershire, the El Dorado of English gardening, invented the first lawnmower, inspired by a contraption used in the manufacturing of velvet. His hand-pushed machine set new standards, and I wish it were still available. Then, toward the turn of the century, a German chemist found the formula for making synthetic fertilizer, which triggered people's lust for even greener grass. Not long after, the inevitable happened and gasoline powered lawnmowers hit the market. From then on it went from bad to worse. In 1940, the introduction of herbicides made expectations spiral to new heights, and that is when the vicious cycle was set in motion. More fertilizers, more herbicides and pesticides, more irrigation, air and water pollution, and more resource depletion. Today, lawns have become big biz. It is bad news for the planet.

This realization puts me into a quandary, just like eating a succulent steak does. I know it would be better for humanity if I did not. I am just as ambivalent about large expanses of green velvet, aware of how costly they are to the environment as well as to our own pocketbook. Clearly, lawns should only be allowed in rainy climates. But what are we others of the dryer regions supposed to do? For nothing is as gratifying to look at and as soft on the feet as a well-kept lawn. How on earth can we wean ourselves off this luxury? I am afraid until someone comes up with a short, soft grass that does not need to be watered and cut regularly—and I don't mean the indoor–outdoor plastic version—we are unlikely to renounce it. So what is to be done? For one thing we could be more tolerant and let in the hoi polloi of quack, timothy, foxtail, and other such *Gramineae* that are not welcome in the polite society of turf grasses. Or we might consider paddocks of grazing sheep instead, which presents us with problems of a different nature. Who is going to shear them when the time comes, and what will we do with the wool, which nobody will buy these days, much less spin? Of course I have composting ideas again...bone meal, after all, is a valuable fertilizer—is wool that different? I'm also trying to reduce the area of lawn

Rocca di San Giorgio near Piacenza was ▶
originally a sixteenth-century military fortification.
It eventually was turned into a villa with a proper
piece of lawn in front of it.

The round *tapis vert* near the entrance of Mount Vernon,
the home of George and Martha Washington in Virginia, U.S.A.

by adding bushes here and subshrubs there. Groundcovers are probably not such a good idea where there is the possibility of snakes. We have them. I know they are the gardener's best friends, but our Italian ones are darn ugly—unlike the ones we had in Katonah, which had a pretty black and yellow design on their back, easy to see when they were sunning themselves on the compost heap and sometimes copulating. Alas, this did not bestow the gift on me that Tiresias got, of changing to the other sex and finding out what that was like. My *Coronella laevis* and *Natrix helvetica*—not poisonous—are mud colored or black, and shock me by their sudden appearance in unexpected places. They like to be off the ground, and occasionally I see one slithering on top of a box hedge or disappearing under a roof, making the expression "a snake in the grass" largely academic. Their shed skins, more than a meter long, can regularly be found between the branches of the many flowering climbers we have.

So if we must have a proper, well-groomed, weed-free lawn, the one I would recommend is one of those clear-cut pieces in a geometric shape, which the French aptly call *tapis vert* or green carpet. Style is added by what contains them: ribbons of flowers, low box hedges, or paths covered with fine gravel from the Loire in a warm beige color. A definite taste projected by a definite will is what characterizes these French lawns, particularly when accompanied by the stern sign "Pelouse Interdite," the tone of which makes me giggle. This dictatorial approach—still under the influence of the Sun King—is currently being changed by the grassroot movement of popular demand, and we now can find alternate signs that say "Pelouse Autorisée." The two notices get swapped at regular intervals as prolonged trampling of the grass destroys it.

A modern alternative for grass is supplied by expanses of pebbles, with flowering plants pushing up through the stones wherever they please. This can be very attractive when the flowers are in bloom. Much of the credit for this interesting style goes to Beth Chatto, one of the grande dames of English gardening. She was among the pioneers to grapple with drought, which hardly was a factor in the British Isles until we woke up to the inconvenient truth that the most distressing new age of climate change is already upon us. If we decide to do something different and are willing to give up the concept of carpeting, we could embark on planting ornamental grasses. I first came across them through the designers Wolfgang Oehme and James Van Sweden, who

Ornamental grasses are an attractive substitute for lawns.

furnished whole gardens with these low-maintenance perennials that need cutting only once a year. Their plumy and feathery seed heads gracefully swaying in the breeze create the illusion of a natural scene, especially when they are planted in large drifts. Echoing the reeds and dune grasses of beaches, they proved to be an inspired choice for seaside gardens and swimming pools. What had begun as a fashionable trend, feeding the gardener's inborn hankering for novelty, turned out to be the perfect answer to our current desire for a naturalized landscape as well as for the need to simplify the maintenance involved. Homeowners had found a way to reduce the area of lawn drastically, or in some cases to throw away the mower altogether. The variety of these ornamental grasses now available has become large and sophisticated. They stay put through the winter, but for a seasonal touch we can combine them with simple flowers like cosmos or lychnis and such, also planted in large swatches. The most original pairing I have encountered is a patch of striped zebra grass interspersed with chartreuse green gladioli—resembling the unexpectedly happy marriage of two serious neurotics.

But this is not where the story of grass ends. It has an afterlife as straw. Interestingly, Ötzi, the iceman and oldest character in history, had some dried grass stuck to his footgear, which allowed modern science some 5,000 years later to determine where he had started out from. Harvesting and storing straw and hay was once a skill—one of the many lost. Haycocks attracted the attention of numerous painters, Millet, Monet, and Van Gogh among them, and the photographer Fox Talbot chose a haystack in the shape of a house as a worthy subject. In some regions—in Romania and Japan for instance—such traditional unusual shapes can still be found.

Hay—different from straw—is used as fodder and tied to a sense of well-being. Once the hay is in, safe and sound, a sense of relief arose in the farming communities of old. I was surprised to learn that in earlier periods of history people had to tighten their belts not in the depth of winter, as I had assumed, but in summer when the grain reserves were likely to run out during the month preceding the harvest. The sight of hay thus spells pleasure and has a distinct connection with wealth. Making hay while the sun shines, the heydays, a hay ride, and so on, are all positive notions. When talking about rich people in our colloquial Swiss dialect we say that they have money like hay. Hieronymus Bosch illustrated this concept most evocatively in his allegorical painting *The Haycart*: a happy couple of lovers sits high up on top of a hay wagon, making merry, singing and playing music, while the populace below the enormous load of hay is absorbed by its daily struggles and tribulations, with some individuals trying to devise a way to clamber up to the top of the heap.

Albrecht Duerer   Hieronymus Bosch

In our living room in Zurich we did not have a Hieronymus Bosch but a painting of two women in gossamer lingerie, resting on what I thought were bales of hay.
It hung above a formal sofa that was covered in a cream and bordeaux striped silk,
much in contrast to the hayloft atmosphere above it, which struck me as somewhat
prickly given the diaphanous garments the two ladies wore. Titled *L'Abandon ou
les Deux Amies*, it was painted by someone called Toulouse-Lautrec. When I grew
wiser and old enough to correct my mistaken interpretation of the background
(and foreground!), my father told me the extraordinary story of how he had been
able to add this masterpiece to his modest collection of impressionist paintings. *Les
Deux Amies* had been brought to his attention by his friend, the art historian Got-
thard Jedlicka, when it was offered for sale in Zurich by a private art dealer at what
must have been a very high price, clearly beyond my father's means. He was neither
a banker nor an industrialist, but a doctor, albeit one of considerable prestige. He
had introduced and established radiology as an independent chair at the University
Hospital of Zurich, and as the head of that department became a world-renowned
cancer specialist. Photographs of 1934 show him as the president of the Internation-
al Congress of Radiology, a dashing young figure in the midst of bearded old sci-

Toulouse Lautrec: *Les Deux Amies*

entists. It was around that time that he, Professor Hans R. Schinz, was approached to give a medical consultation to an anonymous patient in Germany. Since he was unreservedly and passionately anti-German, this was out of the question and he declined. The mysterious request was renewed and he said no again. When he was pestered for the third time, his feathers got ruffled and he decided to rid himself of this bother once and for all by asking an astronomical fee. To his astonishment it was promptly accepted, while arrangements in Germany were speedily made for his trip to Munich to meet with the patient. By now he realized that it had to be someone high up on the political ladder. When he found out that the person in question was none other than Hitler himself, he was thrilled. Intensely curious to see Europe's biggest headache face to face, he also entertained the hope of finding a full-fledged and incurable cancer, in which case the world would be freed of a massive problem. The meeting was brief. Hitler was surrounded by a bevy of doctors and bodyguards. My father was surprised by his short stature, and that he was quaking in his boots with fear and reeked of cheap perfume. Most gratifyingly, Adolf had to obey, open his mouth wide for the professor, and say "Aaaah": the problem was in his throat. The diagnosis was easy; regrettably it was not cancer but nodules on the vocal cords, just as Enrico Caruso, the great Italian tenor, also had suffered from. The disappointing diagnosis notwithstanding, my father nevertheless had the immense satisfaction of admonishing Hitler and saying to him: "I have only one piece of advice to give you: You must stop shouting." Spellbound listener that I was, I would have loved to hear more, but all I remember is that my father chucklingly mentioned that he had made sure to collect his fee in advance. Returning home, he lost no time and bought his Toulouse-Lautrec.

The painting graced our living room throughout my childhood and adolescence. After my father's death we had to sell it. It gave us a nice piece of change to cultivate our gardens with. And though it did not trickle down to have our grandchildren dance all the way to the bank, we did make sure to give them the opportunity of romping around on our own bales of hay.

Dancing on our bales of hay.

The Lure of Flowers

Our formal sex education was undertaken by Pastor Frehner in his preparatory course preceding our confirmation. Curiously, it was the sixth commandment, "Thou shalt not commit adultery," that got him onto the slippery path of having us come to grips with the hard facts of procreation. Further down the road, when he arrived at legitimate connubial bliss, he suggested to the baffled boys in his class that the eager husband not crash through the bedroom door with his brutal animal instincts, but delicately announce his desires by bringing his wife a gift of flowers when coming home from work. I loved the idea and saw my future as a steady stream of exquisite bouquets, spiked with tropical blooms heralding steamy nights of erotic arabesques. But before I could get that vividly imagined parade underway, the 1960s arrived and dispensed with the coy preambles of Protestant ministers. Undisguised sex was here, pure and simple. Gifts of flowers were no longer compulsory. Timid overtures of nosegays and tussie-mussies slipped into the realm of collective memory, where they are shelved next to sentimental albums and Victorian manuals on the language of flowers.

Flowers enthrall us with their form, their color, and their scent. They hypnotize us, a power possibly based on and intensified by their symmetry. We worship the brevity of their lives and use them in abundance on special occasions, underscoring our rituals and celebrating the milestones of life. But these are mere side issues. Flowers were not invented for our delight but as packaging for a plant's reproductive organs: its stamens and its pistils. In terms of evolutionary progress, the invention of sexual reproduction was a stroke of genius. When a flowering plant is fertilized and a second gene pool is drawn into the process, it doubles the likeli-

Stamens and pistils, the reproductive organs of "Madame Galen."

Tuberoses on a Vietnamese altar   A wedding couple in Dalat, Vietnam

hood of useful new traits springing up with every generation. This novel scheme sped up evolution like a turbo injection. To aid and abet this, her goal, nature developed every conceivable bait and trap to bring about pollination. Along with the complex mechanisms for seed dispersal, these devices are often superb pieces of engineering. And since the flower as a whole is not only the packaging but also the advertisement of its content, a wealth of colorful designs was showered on its secondary features too. The role of these petals, sepals, calyxes, and bracts is to attract the insects and other creatures that are essential to the plot. The French cancan of ruffled petals or pink silk slips that flowers put on for the occasion all lead to one point. Many of the markings near the throat of blossoms were actually designed by nature as a landing strip for collaborating insects. Some of them are invisible to the human eye, but not to that of bees: they work like the row of lights on a tarmac that leads the airplane to its gate. The immense variety of designs that evolution bestowed on flowers, be they huge or microscopic, is such that sometimes they don't even look like flowers at all. But with or without a magnifying glass we find them all amazing.

One man who did plenty of looking through loupes was the Swede Carl Linnaeus. His superior view of the natural world and his assiduous plant collecting made him one of the luminaries of the eighteenth century. Convinced that without a clear system of classification, botany was doomed to remain a backward science, he set out to put permanent order into that discipline once and for all. Getting rid of the complications and inaccuracies that clung to the naming of plants in his day, he bestowed a two-word label—a name and surname, so to speak—on every plant, thus establishing a systematic method which was applicable to all plants including those still waiting to be discovered. The idea of binomial nomenclature had been around sporadically, but until then had not found the authority and organizing talent to implement it. Linnaeus was the man who managed to do this in a comprehensive way and with such rigorous consistency that in time—albeit not overnight—it was accepted the world over and remained valid for 200 years. It is still used today. His search for a logical system of classification was based on the insight that a determining trait of every flowering plant was its reproductive organs, namely the fixed number of its stamens and its pistils which can only be distinguished with a powerful magnifying glass. In his *Systema Naturae* he proposed the existence of twenty-three groups or classes (twenty-four if we count the nonflowering plants such as ferns, horsetails, etc.), each of which has a precise combination of reproductive organs as its common denominator. He mischievously called the pistils wives and the stamens husbands, imbedded deep inside the flowers in titillating combinations such as two wives with three husbands or one husband and five wives, and so forth. This revolutionary revelation made people's heads spin and struck them as shockingly scabrous. I would have to reach to a thesaurus to come up with all the smutty insults that were slung at Linnaeus, but his bold new system of identification held up to scrutiny, was simple and practical, and could easily be applied by the botanists who ventured afield, wherever they happened to be. To this monumental task he later added the classification of animals and coined the label *Homo sapiens* for us humans, placing us side by side with the big apes in the class of primates, which did not meet with universal enthusiasm and had some people bristle with indignation. But he possessed that unflappable determination bordering on obstinacy which, along with patience and indefatigability, is the mark of scientists who successfully bring mankind to a new level of knowledge. Since the progress of science is unstoppable we should not be surprised that a massive overhaul of the classification of plants is already in the works. It is now based on DNA and computer science.

Flowers are nature's masterpiece, in function and in looks. Their inner sanctum containing the life-affirming vital organs paired with the fragile beauty of their surrounding petals sets them apart from all else. Since the very essence of flowers is their perishability, we cannot hope for fossils from which paleontologists could glean information. We grope around in the dark for clues about the flowers' earliest days and origins. Apparently they have existed for 150 million years. How or when they added color to their Sunday best will probably remain a riddle forever. Color has got to be

the trump in the flower's hand of cards. The arrival of reds, yellows, and oranges clearly sent new vibrations through a world replete with dusky browns and grayish greens. Red existed in nature but was evanescent: fresh blood oxidizes and sunsets dissolve. A red blossom that could be held in one's hand without the scorching effect of glowing embers must have seemed a miracle. Ditto a bunch of flowers in primary colors.

The most spectacular flower festival I know is the Infiorata in Spello, Umbria. It takes place every year on the Sunday following Corpus Christi, when flowers in the surrounding hills and valleys abound. All the inhabitants participate in the decoration of their streets for the religious procession on Sunday. The scope of the celebration is an ambitious one. The long, uninterrupted cobbled street winding through the medieval town is to be covered with carpets of complex designs, entirely composed of flower petals without the addition of artificial materials. Each tapestry is to be several meters long, leaving a border of paving free on each side for people to file by. Only the archbishop when heading the procession will be allowed to walk on them. As the last flower pickings are rushed into town on Saturday afternoon, young and old begin their work. Nonnas and mammas have already set themselves up on chairs outdoors, with heaps of flowers on their laps and at their feet. Their job is

The Infiorata of Spello in Umbria, Italy

to pull off the petals and sort them by color, snipping them into small and smaller bits, gaily chattering away in the expectation of the marvels to come. They are responsible for the preparation of vast amounts of colorful powders that will serve as the paint from which the carpets are to be fashioned. Some sixty teams of young people are eagerly waiting at the locations they were allotted for the realization of their carefully prepared sketch. As evening falls, the young artists passionately set to work and will continue through the night, hoping to win a prize—an incentive that has been introduced to add some secular excitement. The subject matter of the carpets is often religious—biblical scenes, quotes from the New Testament, Adams and Eves, angels, puttis, and madonnas—or, when not straightforward fantasy, derived from classical paintings. It is tricky work, executed kneeling, crouching, or bending down. But Michelangelo did not have it easy either when painting the ceiling of the Sistine Chapel. I am sure he would have chuckled seeing some of his designs duplicated in flowers. These motifs, and those of many of his contemporaries, are frequently referenced if not copied at this event. Some of the masterpieces only get finished minutes before the gates open to the visitors outside, who throng the town for this famous event when the archbishop, after celebrating Mass, comes out of the church and walks the whole length of the carpeted street, leading the

Part of a flower carpet, Spello ►►

procession while holding his host high, and followed by priests who swing their incense burners and try their best not to ruffle the carpets with their feet. But no matter how careful their steps, the fragile artworks are already beginning to disintegrate. In the course of the day, breezes will scatter the petals further and further, and by the evening the street cleaners with their prosaic vacuum cleaner will have eliminated every trace of these wonders. Sic transit gloria mundi.

Cut flowers do a lot for us in lesser quantities too. At our home in Zurich, my mother, who had been brought up in Naples, indulged her passion for flower arranging every week. Our own harvest from the cutting garden—such as larkspurs, sweet peas, zinnias, or snapdragons—was delivered to the kitchen by the gardener. To fill in gaps when there were lulls between blooming periods, she acquired gloriosa lilies, strelitzias, and other novelties from the various florists downtown. A special room adjacent to the kitchen, known as the office, had a sink and cabinets full of vases, where she rummaged around until she found the clippers, the appropriate container, and the metal porcupine for the bottom of the vase to keep the stems in place. I often stood by and admired her taste and skill. It was a calm, pensive process and the results were always impeccable. Never have I even come close to the airiness and elegance of her creations. The most important ingredient for a perfect bouquet is time, and that she had. Her slender white hands ended in almond-shaped, carefully manicured fingernails; their freshly applied red varnish easily rivaled the fragrance of the spiciest carnations and peachiest of fruits—I could not get enough of it. Yet to many of Zurich's natives her red nails were a cause for moral indignation, if not downright xenophobia. The disapproving remarks and side glances dispensed by the Swiss housewives might perhaps be explained as an aftershock of the sumptuary laws that ruled for long periods in the past and forbade the burghers so many of the finer shades of pleasure, especially those of self-adornment.

Luckily the flowers my mother's beautiful hands arranged did not fall under any such limitation. Somewhat unexpectedly, the sober Protestant north excels at flower decoration when southern Europe offers

Sweet peas from the cutting garden

Flowers from bulbs

much less in that department. The flower shops in Naples were nothing short of pathetic, very much like the ones I first saw in Manhattan in the sixties. Their limited stock consisted of dark, long-stemmed roses, gladioli, chrysanthemums, and religiously white lilies. New York's flower trade was whispered to be in the hands of the Mafia, who obligingly provided a number of funerals for which these appropriately stiff and waxy flowers came in handy. A parallel development in Naples would not be the least bit surprising. But by far the worst deprivation of beauty was experienced in Maoist China, where flower bouquets were considered proof of bourgeois decadence; persons who secretly made them at home were denounced and severely punished. Only red and white carnations were admissible when used for the composition of their leader's effigy and similar patriotic images. At the other end of the rainbow we have Japan's utterly refined relationship to nature, particularly the art of ikebana, the formal flower compositions created according to very strict rules and conveying a message. I was averse to this stilted way of floral displays until our trip to Japan in 1986. We arrived in the Empire of the Rising Sun rattled after endless hours in the air, followed by an unforgettable taxi ride from Osaka to Kyoto to the astonishing soundtrack of a baseball game. The driver, dressed in a spiffy white uniform, was watching it on a TV screen on his dashboard while thundering down the highway. When we finally set foot on terra firma at the Kyoto ryokan inn, the first sight I beheld in a corner near the entrance was a stone vase holding a flower arrangement of shimmering, opalescent beauty. This welcoming and refreshing moment changed my opinion about ikebana in the blink of an eye and transported me like a magic carpet to the realm of Gulliver, whose bizarre travels stayed with us throughout that mind-altering trip.

Many of our likes and dislikes are actually a question of context. I know that my taste is prone to change and that what I fancied yesterday can recede into the background and make room for an object I previously felt negative about. In the garden this recurrent event is frequently tied to seeing a plant in its native habitat, where it looks beautiful, that is to say, in tune with the local sense of esthetics—which in turn may originally have been derived from precisely those plants. It took me a passage to India to reverse my opinion about coxcomb, that weird and woolly thing one even hesitates to call a flower. And it was a visit to the fields of marigolds in Mexico that had me come to terms with their vivid orange color, which often strikes such a discordant note in gardens elsewhere. The arsenal of charms that flowers bewitch us with is vast. They appeal to four of our five senses, which is why we grow them in our gardens in the first place. For visual enjoyment there is not just their color but also their architectural magnificence. My childhood love for columbines has never gone away. Seen in profile, their long hollow spurs dancing in the air are lovely to gaze at, as is the frontal view of their full face: a virtuoso act of nature, especially when bicolors add that extra dimension. Columbines are by no means the only flowers played with, sniffed at, and plucked apart by children, and most likely by our distant ancestors too. That we instinctively search a flower for a scent proves what a vital role odors play. This insight is exploited to its limits by the perfume industry, which is fully aware that fragrance is a sexual ornament and happily cashes in on our most sensuous dreams and desires. As a kid I stuffed lily of the valley blossoms up my nostrils so as not to lose a minute of their delicious emanations, planning to become a perfumer when I grew up.

As for flowers' appeal to our tastebuds, I can sum it up with one word: honey! Though a number of flowers can actually be eaten—deep fried elderberry flowers, day-lily buds, sharp-tasting nasturtium butter, stuffed zucchini blossoms, rose jam, and so on—they are of no importance to nutrition and largely a fad to add variation and color to the table. Ever since la nouvelle cuisine began to over-emphasize presentation and pushed good old-fashioned French food onto the back burner, flowers sneaked onto our plates. But the truth is that whenever I sprinkle violets over the salad or freeze borage blossoms into ice cubes my closest dining companions carefully remove them as if they were flies in the ointment. Occasionally I get carried away and make violet ice cream as an Easter treat, though the confectioner's candied violets work better than what I gather in the garden. We have vast quantities of them. They are escapees from a flower bed in which I had placed the first few, which have long since invaded the grass. When these local Parma violets fill the air with their clouds of perfume I wonder how many people are aware that Stendhal's title *La Chartreuse de Parme* is tied to the colors green and violet as a parallel to *Le Rouge et Le Noir*.

Though the sense of touch does not immediately spring to mind, plants are rich in tactile rewards. Botanical descriptions frequently contain significant references to the quality of surfaces: the backside of a leaf can yield more information than its shape. Flower petals, too, are very varied: thick and waxy or gossamer and fragile. Many have a vaguely rubbery feeling, and touching a petal is as unique a sensation as caressing a horse's nose. Oriental poppies for example, give us a whole slue of tactile sensations: first a hairy bud, which then unfurls its crumpled silky petals like a parachute, and later releases hard, edible seeds from the mature pod. Or it yields the sticky sap that is collected for the production of opium. An impressive sequence of sundry textures from just one plant!

Fragrance ranks high, and its absence in a flower strikes me like some curse out of Greek mythology. Many gardeners make serious compromises for this voluptuous enjoyment, selecting inconspicuous but fragrant blossoms over bigger but unscented ones. White flowers in particular seem to release intense fragrances. They may be compensating for the absence of color, or is that too anthropomorphic an observation? Fascinatingly, some blossoms produce their perfume at a specific time of day, while others only do it in the dark of night. That is yet another theme around which a garden might be designed: clockwork pink.

Given these visceral attractions, it is not surprising that we yearn to grow flowers. They sometimes enter the stage through a side door in the form of a complimentary small seed packet, added by the catalog house to an order of carrots, beets, and beans. So why not try? We follow the instructions on the little envelope and some months later we burst with pride at the sight of the vividly colored zinnia we just produced. How easy this was. Few other plants offer as much color as annual flowers. And we decide to have more. The vegetable patch is often the place where we acquire our basic training. Without meaning to be condescending, it is the kindergarten stage of gardening, where we grow things from seed, learn to keep the lines straight and the beds tidy. A novel task is "thinning out," eliminating the smaller seedlings in each row to give the larger ones the mission to proceed and mature. Democratic principles are not applicable here—we follow the blueprint of natural selection. Most vegetables, with a few exceptions, are annuals, which means that their life cycle is completed in one year with countless seeds left behind to start again after the winter is over. This they do either by themselves or under the care of the gardener, who carefully selects the larger seeds and stores them in appropriately dry conditions. For many enthusiasts, gardening continues contentedly along these lines, which allows them to perfect their skills and expand their repertory with novel varieties and heritage seeds.

◄ A perfect peony

For others, the initial vegetable garden turns out to be the springboard for bigger and better things: floriculture! It comes, however, with a caveat: growing flowers is labor intensive. Annuals need seeding, thinning out, and should we desire a bushier plant they have to be pinched back, unless we aim for a long-stemmed piece of perfection for use in flower arrangements or to enter into a competition. Perennials seem easier at first, deceptively so. Most taller flowers, such as peonies and delphiniums, require staking, their supports deftly concealed; this is only possible if done at the right time and not as an afterthought when they are already tall and bushy. All this takes skill, patience, and time, plus copious watering and rich dirt.

Giving in to the urge to grow flowers, we soon handle not just annuals but biennials too, hollyhocks, foxgloves, Canterbury bells, clary sage, which bloom and set seeds during their second year and then die. Maybe on account of their slower growth they are sturdier and present us with a prolonged blooming period. They also have a way of presiding over many smaller blossoming things. No wonder, since they had a whole year to prepare for their moment of splendor. All the ones I have or had are potent self-seeders too. Once we establish the first stand we are likely to encounter them somewhere else in the garden thereafter, in a place of their own choosing, possibly as far away as the roadside. Hollyhocks are even able to grow

Traditions upheld: Amish children on a visit
to Longwood Gardens in Pennsylvania, U.S.A.

roots in the cracks of the pavement. A few vegetables are biennials too, namely cabbages and turnips, a lot less exciting than the poisonous foxglove or the hairy clary sage. On the whole, the pace of biennials suits me perfectly.

Bulbs, rhizomes, tubers, and corms are another tempting category. You know what you can count on. After all, it is a real object we stick into the soil and not some tiny seeds with the tricky tendency to dribble through our fingers into the wrong spots. Bulbs hide out underground a good part of the year. That is also where they form new plants without the interference of sexual reproduction. Once they start growing they acquire their proud stance from the erect stems that often bear just a single flower, as is the case with many daffodils and tulips. Their bladelike leaves seem only of secondary interest until the flowers fade, but then survive to the end of the cycle. Their task is to nourish the bulb hidden down below and prepare it for the following year before they too die down, in an unattractive but inevitable way.

The height tulips and daffodils attain is accurately listed in catalogs, along with their color and the peak of their blooming period: early, middle, or late. This detailed information makes them the perfect choice for pattern planting in predeter-

Eliza Doolittles, from left to right: Istanbul, Saigon, Hanoi, Ljubljana

mined color schemes. Battalions of them can be seen in show gardens and public parks where they appear like colorful soldiers standing at attention. Daffodils and tulips are the flowers we think of first when bulbs are mentioned; together with lilies they form a triumvirate that is universally liked. Judging by the countless variations currently available, they have attracted breeders like a magnet—sometimes with appalling results. The double blossoms of some daffodils, for example, cause such confusion that we do not know any more what's what—and nor do the bees; they do not work double flowers. The goal for many breeders seems to be to get as far away from the norm as possible: bravura at the expense of good taste.

The temptations that bulbs or rhizomes have in store for us could easily fill a whole page. We are faced with *Sandersonia*, *Eremurus*, *Crocrosmia*, *Alstroemeria*, *Tulbaghia*, and a host of others—I have not even mentioned irises, anemones, and dahlias yet. Plus, as stated at the outset, we know what we'll get, unless the packer at the catalog house made a mistake. At least we can count on their size: small bulbs make small flowers and big bulbs bigger ones. The bulbs themselves tell you how deep they should be planted. The rule is two-and-a-half times the height of the bulb. I prefer to see them growing informally, tucked away under a shrub or in drifts as is their wont in

native woodlands and meadows. Irises, on the other hand, get a front seat preferably in carefully chosen colors, or else are selected to join a mixed border. Their rhizomes are planted like a duck in the water: half above and half below the ground.

My floral graduation, however, approached when I discovered the treasure trove of perennials. These herbaceous hardy plants make up the bulk of flower gardens and die down to the ground in winter. Before buying them, we need to find out when exactly they bloom, whether in the spring, summer, or fall. Since in some cases that splendid period may be quite short, we want to consider the quality of their foliage, usually present from April to October. I gathered my initial knowledge through the perusal of nursery catalogs. There were the gorgeously illustrated ones from Wayside Gardens in South Carolina, while White Flower Farm's catalog formerly had no photographs but prided itself on its sophisticated descriptions that made you feel as if you were a member of a literary club. But even here we have to

▲ The spontaneous garden of a Tudor mansion
in Surrey, England

watch out, for just as flowers devised endless ruses to attract visiting insects, catalog writers are equally eager to trap us for their selling purpose. Wishful thinking turns us into gullible buyers who are willing to believe that a particularly uncommon lavender will bloom from May to July, when what is really meant is that it will flourish for barely three weeks during that period depending on your garden's zone.

When, after the first two years of growing perennials, I realized that I could move these plants around like furniture in a room, nothing could hold me back from adding more beds and borders, and filling the trunk of my car to the brim whenever I passed a nursery that had choice material. Fall became as busy a time as spring, for that is the time when overgrown perennials have to be lifted, divided, replanted, and watered. Thus my garden got richer and richer, with leftovers to give away as well, and my dream of a flower bed where everything was lush and gloriously blooming at the same time came within sight in the U.S. Many of us only became acquainted with the cottage garden when it found its way into our vocabulary as a fashionable label rather than a clear definition. We saw it as a sort of picturesque hotchpotch, a none-too-coordinated medley of flowers, the legacy of English country folks with a distinctly green thumb. Its great appeal for us is its casual style and its smallish size, which has to be manageable for a single individual.

The original cottage garden, however, would not qualify as the delight with which we associate it today. It began as an untidy patch in front of a laborer's shack, where humble esculents like turnips and carrots were planted to add some basic food to the hard struggle that was the tenant's life. None of those charming roses clambering over fences or delicate flowers adorning nooks and crannies! These features were a later development when, with growing prosperity, craftsmen and artisans acquired a particular fondness for their small gardens, keeping a close eye on them from their looms or workbenches near the window. Some of these hobby gardeners eventually became florists, who specialized in cultivating flowers and engaging in competitions. This raised their small enclosures to a more decorative level and inspired Gertrude Jekyll to become a scholar of the cottage garden. The revival of her spirit in 1970s America was due to the expiration of the copyright of her books. Publishers competed to secure themselves the reprinting rights to her fine writing and in the process reawakened her pictorial style in horticulture. Commerce is the mother of all things. Until then her name was largely unknown in the U.S., and sometimes confused with Mr. Hyde's alter ego. The

Nasturtiums: easy and heat tolerant ▲

Charleston Manor in Sussex, once the home of Vanessa Bell and Duncan Grant

A roadside cottage garden in England

Claude Monet's painterly garden in Giverny, France

A flowerbed composed entirely of half-hardy and hardy annuals at its summer peak in Normandy.

Arley Hall, Cheshire, has the oldest herbacious borders in England.

A rock garden at Ninfa in central Italy

distinction made between the two Jekylls incidentally lies in their pronunciation. Known as the trailblazer of floriferous garden scenes in harmonious hues, the formidable Gertrude is invoked as the godmother of many flower gardens to this day. Her large herbaceous borders—her own in Somerset was 200 feet long—became all the rage as a reaction to the stiff and jazzy flower beds that were the prevailing choice of Victorian high society. But to our modern eyes her masterpieces would not have looked as casual as they must have then. Her plans, drawn up for hundreds of herbaceous perennials, were painstakingly planned at her desk, leaving nothing to chance. They addressed every aspect of height, color coordination, and sequence of bloom, and how to have something bloom at any given moment, all of which required maximum maintenance, and skilled maintenance at that. As some of the English country houses of her day had as many as fifty gardeners, that was not a problem—which is tantamount to saying that her spectacular borders were about as natural as a Broadway musical.

In matters of taste it is almost impossible not to be influenced in one way or another. Even when we foolishly pride ourselves on our independent thinking, we are in the hands of other forces and sometimes unaware that we are caving in to the trends of the moment. Some of it is rooted in commerce, by what is available in the marketplace, in nurseries, galleries, or fashion shops. I remember a huge chart on a wall at the headquarters of Conde Nast's *House & Garden* magazine on Madison Avenue where the arrivals and exits of fashionable colors were posted and regularly adjusted like the markers on the maps of battlefields. Coming in from the left were the hot new numbers that were likely to become tomorrow's bestsellers, which, when they had seen their day, such as avocado colored kitchen appliances, were ushered out on the right. The impact of colors on the human psyche is a given, and their cargo of symbolisms have turned them into carriers of nonverbal communication. Purple conveyed status and nobility in Roman antiquity until cardinal red took over, thereafter undergoing various transformations. Today, red alerts us to danger, signifies passion, or brings good luck, depending on what country you are in. A big change of pace was brought about when, in the nineteenth-century, modern chemistry amplified the color range, while the most recent shift in our perception is due to the silver screen and its TV equivalent. Against our will we have gotten used to its exaggerated tints and clashing hues. Currently, the Photoshop computer program with its tempting saturation button is the main culprit for alienating us from reality, seducing us with the arrival of never-before-experienced intensified colors—which the paint manufacturers are now happy to produce to satisfy the consumers' ravenous appetite for more and stronger. What can possibly be next?

Inevitably, where distinctions of refinement are made, snobbism puts a foot in the door. Horticulture is a time-honored vehicle for the disdain aired by the upper vis-à-vis the middle class. Just read Jane Austen. But what arrives in the garden as a coveted novelty will soon experience wider distribution and run the risk of ultimately ending up as a cliché. Colors and color combinations of flowers in particular fall into the realm of sophistication. A white wisteria purportedly is proof of a high-minded gardener, whereas a blue wisteria is, well, just a wisteria. Having a properly labeled "Amethyst" or "Black Dragon" makes it a mitigating circumstance, but still, it ain't white. Similarly, the pairing of pale blues and pinks in a mixed border was an absolute must for decades, whereas the choice of red and yellow, especially when growing side by side, was regarded as esthetically troublesome and turned us into vulgarians. I am not sure if these ideas are still whirling around, but I know that some plants will always be in and others out. Semiramis in all likelihood turned up her nose at the mundane stuff that was growing down below near the roadside. I think it is a human feature that just cannot be eliminated, even if we find it silly. Old styles and cultivars are thrown out and new ones come in. It's the way the world works. Good taste cannot be taught and is best acquired through osmosis and experience. Looking at other people's gardens will hone our critical faculties and may prompt us to copy what we find convincing. Gardens that stay the same for years frequently have us shift gear to introduce some novel refreshment. Flowers certainly are an easy method to effect such worthwhile changes.

Wedding or funeral? Park Avenue, New York City, U.S.A.

In praise of Shrubs and Climbers

There comes a time in life when we are not prepared to wait for a tree to mature. We suddenly discover the existence of shrubs to which we hitherto had not paid much attention. This impatience is typical for the later phases of our life, but also rears its head when we move to a new place and find ourselves confronted with a backyard that is only sparsely planted—which incidentally may be a blessing in disguise. I would hate to have to start a garden by ripping out a predecessor's tamarisks and rhododendrons, which might give me bad karma. A clean slate is not a bad thing when you know what to write on it. Shrubs are basically trees with several trunks and therefore grow much faster. They have other wondrous qualities too, but their potential for speedy growth and functional use must account for the larger half of bushes bought. Screening out the place next door is a spontaneous impulse that even devout philanthropists are prone to. Mankind is good. It's the neighbors that are not up to snuff. They probably want to see as little of us as we of them, strutting around in questionable garments or even totally without. A green division of large bushes is therefore welcomed by both parties and seems less brutal than the finality of a brick wall. The question tends to be who gets to choose the plants and who will pay for them.

The difference between trees and shrubs is not as iron-clad as one might think, since many trees can become shrubs, just as some shrubs can be turned into small trees. The first is not always a matter of choice. The historic January of 1985 when most olive groves of Tuscany were decimated by a sudden unprecedented plummeting of temperature to minus 27 degrees Celsius lives forth in the collective memory of Italians. Thousands of the trees had to be cut down. Life eventually sprang up again from their roots, giving them a

Sprouting hazelnut

◄ *Ceanothus Concha* or Californian lilac

new chance as shrubs. True, this is a depressing compromise for a tree with the potential to become 800 years old, with an immense, gnarled trunk. But being alive is better than not and it beats being turned into a salad bowl or a cutting board. Or even worse, disposed of as firewood. Conversely, the likes of *Laurus nobilis, Vitex agnus-castus*, and *Parrotia persica* are shrubs that can become tall and treelike when grown in a mild climate with sufficient sun and precipitation. I doubt my *Arbutus unedo* will ever become trees. Drought puts a lid on them and I shall keep them multi-stemmed and bushy. Bushes offer themselves without the stiffness and immobility of trees, and unlike them do not overshadow other plants, reducing them to bit players. As valuable contributors to the basic green structure they lend volume as well as height to the picture we want to create. When growing flowers seems too labor-intensive they are a viable alternative. One of their attractions is that they carry their ornamental assets at eye level and are apt to give off beguiling scents right under our nose. By now I consider it a treat not to have to stoop down to admire their blossoms, since so much of the work in the garden is done bending and crouching, or even, with advancing age, crawling on one's belly.

There is no simple formula for which shrubs to plant. The permutations of climate, soil, and the hundreds of individuals to select from make it an enticing challenge. Compare it to doing a crossword puzzle, but one that allows for more than a single answer, leaving room for a certain amount of creativity. To bring order to the rich palette of possibilities, shrubs are grouped in numerous ways. Other than the obvious classification according to size, which also includes subshrubs, there is the separation into deciduous and evergreens. The latter are divided into conifers and broadleaved evergreens. Since names are not always foolproof, evergreen leaves can also be purple, grey, yellow, or variegated, and may include some with foliage that is feathery and narrower than what the term broadleaf would imply. To further blur the edges, some varieties are listed as semi-evergreens: they shed part of or all their leaves depending on the rudeness of the climate, become confused by cold spells, and ape the behavior of deciduous plants, letting go of all their leaves simultaneously. All evergreens, by the way, rejuvenate themselves and usually do so gradually. Should yellowing leaves appear on your shrubs and cause you instant panic, it is probably not a sign of sickness but rather part of the normal process, as new ones will form in due course to replace them. While in the depth of winter their curled, drooping leaves look dark and funereal, no sooner is a whiff of spring in the air than they perk up and put things right again. Their ready-made framework gives us a head start that is a huge advantage in regions that can count on mild winters.

◄ The infinite palette of shrubs

In my personal notes to date, I have a category called the "unkillables," often regarded by others with contempt rather than with the respect that their unflappability should command. Cotoneasters and pyracanthas are among them, as well as the ubiquitous *Prunus laurocerasus*. Privets are equally sturdy growers as the above, and like them are often used for hedges. "Too banal," says the snob, "why not yew?" But if you garden on difficult soil, you soon leave such judgments behind. Our Italian garden abounds in rather mundane plants because they fare well even in adverse conditions, and that is why they please. Not that I do not hanker after the rare and distinguished, which I sometimes manage to acquire in distant nurseries in Switzerland or on the French Riviera. But not all of these subjects have professed great enthusiasm for their new location. So we are happy with hawthorns, hollies, brooms, smoke bushes, mock oranges, and lilacs that are tough enough to stand poor ground and have defined the landscape surrounding us long before we arrived. The result is that our garden in Italy is a slightly polished version of the wild vegetation of the northern Apennines, borrowing what it can from richer neighborhoods, which is possible as long as we provide these newcomers with the water they feel entitled to.

Another group of happy campers are the so-called subshrubs. Many of them are aromatic herbs of Mediterranean origin, to name the sages, artemisias, and lavenders for example. They want full sun and dry, poor soil: music to my ears. Destined to become woody and brittle by the fall, they should be cut back sharply in early spring to retain their compact growth. In the north they die back by themselves, without secateurs or a return guarantee, so they have to be replaced periodically. Luckily for the nursery trade, their romantic Mediterranean connotation and their strong and often spicy fragrances persuade many gardeners to reach into their pockets and unrepentantly replace them year after year. Just as it is in real estate, the name of the game in horticulture is location, location, location. And since not everybody lives in those miracolous places where an almost unlimited number of plants can be grown—Santa Barbara, California, or parts of Yunnan, to mention two—the tantalizing list of plants found in catalogs and encyclopedias

Lupinus arboreus

Detail of a box parterre planted with sea lavender and lavender.

is soon whittled down to the happy few that our respective climate and soil will permit us to grow. Thus we try to decide which shrubs to have a closer look at. There are shrubs that thrive in blazing sun and those that live in deep shade or need dappled shade instead, or can only survive on wet terrain. There are drought-resistant shrubs, spiny ones that discourage vandalism, shrubs good for hedges of whatever kind, or others with aromatic foliage, fragrant flowers, ornamental fruits. And then of course we can choose from the vast offering of flowering shrubs or from those that take on bright colors in the fall.

The factor that had the biggest impact on my choices when we moved to Italy is the necessity to know a plant's dependence on the soil's pH factor. The acid-loving versus the alkaline-friendly factions are like two opposing teams, and currently my sworn allegiance is to the ones that tolerate alkalinity. I felt really sorry for myself on arrival in our Italian Arcadia when getting acquainted with its poor and clayish soil and realizing that henceforth I had to forgo *Fothergilla gardenii*, *Kalmia latifolia*, *Enkianthus campanulatus*, and some smaller calcifuguous plants like ferns and hostas. Many hailing from Japan had felt thoroughly at home in our American garden surrounded by native trees and shrubs. The phrases "lime tolerant" or "not particular to

soil" are blessings I now appreciate. But I should not be unfair, because the opposite happened too: *Philadelphus coronarius* (a north Italian native), *Ceratostigma plumbaginoides*, and oakleaf hydrangeas are thriving. It almost seems to be a formula: what did well in my American gardens has a hard time in our Italian soil and vice versa. Luckily some plants do not care if the soil is sour or sweet, so I simply hope for the best, all the while listening to what other practitioners have to say. Their opinions frequently differ: horticulture is not an exact science. An expert gardener, having acquired ample knowledge, will never tell you that you must do this or should do that. At most he will offer some kindly advice, beginning with "You might want to try..." since he knows full well that every garden is site-specific and has its own distinct qualities, which may differ even from a seemingly similar one nearby.

One thing is sure: if you want the blossoms of your lace cap hydrangeas to be blue, or if you are a fan of azaleas, or a fanatic for rhododendrons, you cannot ignore the pH value of your ground. Acid soil and damp air are the indisputable requirement of most members of the *Ericaceae* family, to which rhododendrons belong. They have to be assured of a pH value of 6 or thereabouts. The reader may have noticed my ambivalence towards rhododendrons and their loud cousins, the azaleas. This is not entirely capricious on my part, nor is it a case of sour grapes. The rhododendron's starring role is so distinct that Western gardening could be divided into the pre-rhododendron era and what came after. When exploration of Himalayan flora began in 1820, the first introductions opened the door to a steady stream of imports from that new part of the world. Before long, the creation of novel hybrids started up and continues to keep the rhododendron passion fueled to the present day. Harold Hillier dedicates forty-six pages to these darlings while roses get a measly twelve pages. True, this can be justified inasmuch as the richness and variety of the 800 species of rhododendrons is unparalleled by any other family. They seduce us with their magnificent blossoms that beckon in an almost unlimited range of vivid colors to the most delicate, subtle hues and pure whites. Many of them are remarkable for their distinguished habit of growth and strongly defined foliage, features which to the connoisseur are every bit as important as their flowers. The majority of them are evergreen. So there is a lot to be said for the members of this clan. Add to it that they originated in the moist environment and dappled shade of the mountain forests of Burma, Sikkim, and Yunnan, which made them very eligible for the cool, mild parts of western Europe and the northwest coast of the U.S. and New Zealand. Small wonder that they simply swamped the gardens of the Western world.

◄ Japanese maples at New York Botanical Garden

Their main problem is that they, along with azaleas, are often planted out of place. The terracotta pots filled with shocking pink azaleas that are scattered throughout some Italian Renaissance gardens are the visual equivalent of the chalk's screech on blackboard. Stourhead in England is another example where rhododendrons rub some viewers the wrong way. The purist wants to experience the scene as it was originally intended, that is to say as a pastoral landscape in green and muted colors like the paintings of Le Lorrain. So the question arises: Should places like Stourhead and its equivalents not be maintained as the finest example of their kind, unmarred by new introductions? During my early garden photography trips in England with my friend Tessa Traeger, we a priori ruled out the places that named rhododendrons and azaleas as their highlights. We were after a different esthetic, that of humble cottage gardens, or else the jewels in the crown of English gardening like Sissinghurst, Great Dixter, Cranborne Manor, and so forth. Rhododendrons simply did not turn us on. Now, decades later, I have to admit that some gardens dedicated to rhododendrons and azaleas do exist that are worth looking at. I am thinking of the late Sir Peter Smithers' steep hillside above Lake Lugano mimicking impressions of the Far East, or the pink vales of Villa Carlotta on Lake Como, which was Queen Victoria's wedding gift to one of her daughters. Amazing when at their peak, these places give us the odd impression that is an equivalent to what gifted writers present us with when they create a pastiche: a story told in the style of another author. They are acts of bravura. Early on, in Katonah, as a greenhorn, I got away with planting a *Rhododendron schlippenbachii* at the foot of a drystone wall and surrounding its base with native *Trilliums grandiflorum* and *Mertensia virginica*, treating myself to some pink and blue American rococo. It sort of worked as the rhododendron was the deciduous kind, its lovely, pale pink blooms appearing before the leaves. Normally not intent on going back to my old haunts, it is a spot I would not mind seeing again in order to decide if I should remain grateful to Baron von Schlippenbach for his discovery, enhanced by my addition of that heavenly blue of the Virginia cowslips which is the most satisfying tint in the universe.

▲ The kiosk arrived in Europe from the Ottoman Empire, the hydrangeas from Asia.

Occasionally, before dozing off at night, I finding myself magically transported to a cool and mild climate with acid soil, where I perforce will have a rhododendron garden. I project stunning effects with large swatches of colors, inspired by the washes of abstract painters. Since my garden dreams never stray far from practical considerations, I am greatly helped in my musings by the surface rooting habit of rhododendrons, which allows the designer to lift up the designated shrubs with their compact roots and move them to another spot, so that during the next season you can decide if the new composition pleases you. Their tolerance for being transplanted surely adds to their popularity. Azaleas so far have not entered my mental playground. Their reds are too one-dimensional and their whites too uniform. It seems I'm not the only one with this opinion, for I have heard of Japanese esthetes who have the flower buds removed before their azaleas begin to bloom so as to enjoy the bushes just as a green form—which is clearly beyond my ken.

Acid soil-loving azaleas and rhododendrons

Clipped shrubs and hedges tell us where a garden begins (or ends).

Jardin de l'Evêché de Castres, by Le Notre

The steady clipping of the pruning shears is better applied to hedges, formal hedges especially, that thrive under the constant correctional cuts. For the last 2,000 years, *Buxus*, or box, has lent itself admirably to being shaped and is one of the garden's finest elements, not just to define and separate outdoor living spaces or encase flowerbeds but often to form the heart of the ornamental garden itself. Intricate knot gardens and complex parterres got pride of place in classical gardens, while the playful art of topiary, which took off already in Roman days—the gardener was called *topiarus*!—has never lost its humorous potential. Gradually, many other plants were found to respond favorably to being clipped: most notably yew, but also rosemary, ilex, privet, hyssop, germander, and so on. Trees such as hornbeams and beeches also can be used as formal hedges. But for these the shears are not the necessity that they are for *Buxus sempervirens*. My parents grew such a specimen in our courtyard out of botanical interest. Never tended

Topiaries in England, Ireland, Wethersfield Estate
in New York, and Green Animals Topiary Garden in Rhode Island, U.S.A.

165

Camellias originated in the Far East and conquered the world.

but left to grow as it wished, it was as unsightly a plant as I ever saw. The question of whether its craving for sun was stronger than its desire to be pruned was answered when I saw some olive trees near Rome, untouched by human hands. They looked unspeakably shabby and I bet they did not fruit well either. Shearing or pruning is essential to the performance of *Buxus* and olives. By and large, most shrubs benefit from being looked after with secateurs to some degree, groomed if not pruned, a slight haircut here and there, some thinning out, and dead wood removed whenever necessary. Control of height can become more of a chore when shrubs grow higher than we reckoned. It is a recurrent problem in my garden, whereas the process called rejuvenation is one where humans put one over on nature. It is a surgical massacre that is applied to hedges, which get cut back on the whole front side one year and on the back side the year after so as to spur them into thicker growth. This is not to be undertaken without professional advice as it could turn you into a butcher or a murderer. The when is as crucial as the how.

We also have to know our onions when it comes to choosing the exact place where we want to plant our shrubs, because they will be there for a long time. Try and acquaint yourself with the plants in real life before you buy them, so that you get to know the individuals in their various seasonal guises beforehand. Some of them refuse to be moved once established, and therefore must be sited at the outset where they show themselves to their best advantage. You want to be sure, for instance, to position a *Magnolia sieboldii* on rising terrain so that its gloriously white nodding flowers can be viewed from below. Purple-leaved shrubs such as *Cotinus coggygria* "Purpureus" benefit from being backlit by the rising or the setting sun: an eastern or western exposure is preferable to a north-facing wall. And to get the maximum effect of a fragrant *Viburnum carlesii* it should be planted near a window that is frequently opened, while others that can cause allergies or are magnets to wasps are banned from areas near the house, terrace, or swimming pool. There also exist some weirdoes in the world of shrubs for which

A camellia market
in Dali, Yunnan

A green border with hydrangeas in Normandy

we simply may never find a perfect spot. I am thinking of *Corylus avellana* "Contorta" or "Harry Lauder's Walking Stick," a plant so bizarre that it looks best after shedding its leaves, at which point it resembles a bouquet of upside-down corkscrews. And yet I once saw it superbly placed in the wintery, cloistered courtyard of a French monastery, where the naked branches echoed the decorative stonework of the Gothic arches. I dare say this is a hard act to follow when it comes to supplying a suitable background.

Botanical gardens base their plantings on didactics rather than on esthetics. They sometimes group the plants according to their place or continent of origin, or by the habitats they favor. At the Planting Fields Arboretum on Long Island we can stroll through a synoptic garden of ornamental shrubs suited to the local climate. Someone with a literary bent had the peculiar idea to plant them in alphabetical order, which the plants themselves did not notice, but is of help to us when we have to guess the names of what we are looking at. A piece of good advice is to step back and look at a shrub with an unbiased eye when it is not in bloom. For that is how we see it most of the time, unless we live in the tropics. It needs to have beauty of form and leaf. In a small garden a shrub may be chosen as a focal point, and it certainly pays to select a type with a protracted flowering season. A plant collector may want to exhibit his or her foreign treasures in a more prominent place, a group of rare eucryphias for instance, that elusive genus of Chilean origin demanding a mild climate and acid soil. Another possibility is to dedicate an area to shrubs with particular appeal—distinguished foliage perhaps. Or to create a long-term parking space for that motley crew of bushes you just happen to have hanging around because you never found the right place for them. These questionable chaps are best bunched up and relegated to the periphery. In England this so-called shrubbery is the place where Sherlock Holmes occasionally finds an important clue to the crime, or on a lucky day maybe even another corpse—a fringe benefit as it were.

Smoke bush or *Cotinus coggygria* ▶
is fairly drought resistant.

Witch hazel (*Hamamelis vernalis*) in autumn

A *Campsis radicans* clings to this Alsatian house.
Vineyard in the background.

The most exciting plants to me are climbers: upwardly mobile. They have many characteristics in common with their brothers or sisters, the shrubs, but with that unbeatable extra of ambition. Some are exuberant, rambunctious, and overpowering, others tentative, timid, and docile. Whether they pose as coy or self-assured, we can choose among the hardy and the tender, between annuals and perennials, as well as between evergreen and deciduous. Some are early risers, others slow starters, some late bloomers, but whatever their special features, they are head and shoulders above the rest. They not only know where they want to go, they also have the wherewithal to get there. Most impressive is the sure instinct with which they direct their young shoots toward the post or wall that is destined to become their support. Having grasped it, they reach higher and higher, some by gripping or clutching the surface with the barnacle-like force of stem roots or aerial roots. Others use the calligraphic flourishes of tendrils to deftly weave themselves into branches or trellises. Yet others twine themselves with single-minded determination around the poles the gardener drove into the ground for them. Chinese wisteria winds itself clockwise around its support, while Japanese wisteria insists on doing it counterclockwise. I did not expect to encounter nationalism among plants and would have thought they were above that. What their wily ways suggest, however, is that plants have an innate intelligence. Among the oldest of all climbers, I like to think, is the grapevine; its sweet cluster of fruit must have preceded the apple as an object of desire, and vineyards possibly arrived before orchards. The remarkable vitality of *Vitis vinifera* asserts itself underground too, where its roots can attain the astonishing length of twenty meters and more. This tenacity enables it to grow even in truculent soils often too poor for other crops. Or as that Burgundy winegrower remarked: "Si notre terre n'était pas parmis les plus riches, elle serait la plus pauvre." When we had settled into our Italian nest but were still undecided what to do with a piece of a bare hillside where potential soil erosion had to be addressed, Franco, our farmer, persuaded us to put in a small vineyard. Devised as a piece of landscaping, it is as decorative as it is functional. The 350 plants, half Bonarda and half Barbera grapes, cover the steep slope with spectacularly neat lines and are a joy to behold, even before we get to taste the 500 bottles of red table wine that they yield most years.

Having gotten off on the wrong foot when attempting to plant some large-leaved kiwis and a Dutchman's pipe, the Boston ivy was a very different story. Even before the restoration of the villa was finished, I had tried to dig a hole at the bottom of a large wall of a stone building destined for tools and a tractor. The cementlike ground was much too hard for a spade and I had to resort, no joke, to a hammer and chisel until I had hollowed out a small cavity no bigger than the size of a melon. It was by all standards inadequate and not fit as a planting hole. But I was in a hurry and had no choice, so I just stuck the straggly little *Parthenocissus* spp. into the pocket with two handfuls of peat moss and whatever soil I could scratch up nearby, then watered it copiously. I felt rather ashamed of my shoddy work, convinced that nothing would come of it and the poor plant would die in short order. Not so. It took off and in a mere couple of years covered the whole facade of the two-story building with its bright green leaves that turn into an electrifying red come autumn. On the north side of the same building I put in six or eight ivies. Waist high when I bought them, they came in six-inch pots and had a stick holding them upright. Due to the favorable growing conditions and friable soil in that spot they rapidly took and immediately produced new shoots at eye level. But these obstinately refused to attach themselves to the wall as any normal ivy would. For the first two years, while the Boston ivy raced ahead, they hung loose, having been helped by a friendly soul who laboriously fiddled with nails, hooks, and strings. Finally, someone told me I should give the plants a fresh start in life by cutting them all the way down to the ground. This was radical advice but, amazingly enough, after I had done it and the new tips were born, they gripped the wall without further ado. The moral here seems to be that too much help is counterproductive. The potted toddlers had gotten accustomed to the extra help, became lazy and refused to function on their own. It left me wondering where caring ends and spoiling be-

The splendid wisterias of the late ►
Sir Peter Smithers above Lake Lugano

gins...and not just in the garden. Another thing experience has taught me is that a clean cut is a must. Never yank. Just think what a surgeon does to the human body. He never yanks. Nor should you.

Considering how much insight can be gained from these relatively plain climbers, chosen for their foliage, imagine the pleasure to be had from those we grow for their flowers and their fragrance. Here in Italy I have more than a dozen, and every year I am searching for yet another spot to accommodate my latest acquisition. On these pages I have to limit myself and can give the reader only a short list of the winners. For sheer flower power I must start my list with the perfectly named morning glory, which surely is a winner of many awards as well as self-congratulations. It is a good choice for beginners since it is relatively easy to grow and makes masses of perfectly round blooms the size of small saucers, which are of such a pure blue that you will not be the least bit surprised when an ignorant passer-by leans over your garden fence to inquire what that amazing thing is. Having given its splendid performance all morning, it feels entitled to close shop in the middle of the afternoon. Which is why it would be a mistake to grow it on the arbor underneath which you plan to spend your sunset hours. But if you did, never mind, for it is an annual and you get another chance next spring when you can seed it in another place, this time speeding up its germination by filing the tips of the black seeds with a nail file, which you would not have dared to do the first time round. A perennial climber with equally showy flowers is the fiery red *Campsis x tagliabuana* "Madame Galen." She may make you wait for a couple of years, but from then on reliably blooms for years to come. Every so often I remove her wilting flowers and cut off the woody seedpods that begin to form. Should you have the luck to find a specimen already in flower when offered for sale, and see a burnt orange one with a golden throat, grab it and treasure it. The size and the luminosity of its flowers is what sets it apart from its forbears, the species *Campsis radicans*, and it is quite a pretty plant too, with smaller blossoms. It has impressive vigor, can grow in very hot spots, attracts wasps, and is able to eat up whole buildings on account of its rampant suckering habit.

Undisputed king among climbers is the wisteria. Books can and have been written about this regal plant. It reaches great height and a ripe old age, proving this with massive, often twisted trunks. I decided to grow a wisteria on the south facade of our villa, for it can withstand great summer heat while its foliage remains a pleasant green. The potent perfume of its white blossom is so strong that we sometimes prefer to keep the windows closed when it blooms. A word of caution regarding the color of its abundant flowers is appropriate here. If you buy a wisteria without reliable information of its precise name, you run the risk of ending up with a plant of a nondescript

Clockwise from left: *Campsis x tagliabuana* "Madame Galen"
White wisteria in Old Westbury Gardens, New York
Campsis radicans eats up a whole house in Italy.

bloodless blue that soon fades to a repulsive shade of gray when what you want, and can have, is beautifully saturated blue, lilac, or pink tints. Given my record of acquiring plants of mistaken identity, I would not dream of touching a wisteria, or certain other shrubs for that matter, without having verified its looks when in flower at a nursery first. Not even the labels are necessarily always correct. For those who can have the space, a private nursery patch is a good idea so that the various subjects can be studied before they are set out in their final spot. This may take a little patience and some self-discipline, but is well worth the wait. Wisterias also need to be controlled by being cut back with both winter and summer pruning. I love to edit its structure, for while the stems can become seriously twisted around each other, developing a non-strangulating skeleton seems a better course. Developing the basic coordinates is part of the fun of growing climbers, though we are sometimes in for setbacks. When pruned or handled the wrong way, plants can respond by sulking for two full years.

Originally I had tried to stay away from shrubs and climbers imported from Asia, favoring the concept of native plants. But having had no luck with honeysuckles, I early on switched to what in the meantime seems to have become everybody's favorite: *Trachelospermum jasminoides*. Its leathery evergreen foliage and strongly scented white flowers have swept away all memories of my unhappy *Loniceras halliana*. Easily seduced by fragrances, I began to appreciate scents even more after I learnt that the total loss of olfactory sensation can lead to depression and even suicide. No wonder then that all a nursery lady has to do is wheedle a fragrant little flower under my nose to have me buy it and embark on yet another plant adventure. I am partial not just to many perfumes but to dubious odors as well, and sometimes reminisce nostalgically about the potent wafts that skunks leave behind on their American trails. One of my climbers is a *Bignonia capreolata*, a distant relative of Madame Galen and undoubtedly looked down on by her for the uncouth odor of its maroon and yellow flowers (while Madame has no fragrance whatsoever), which catalog writers slyly liken to the aroma of chocolate—a willful distortion, for to the discerning nose the scent is not of chocolate but of broth. It is a plant I highly recommend for its rich green foliage during the hottest and driest summer months, and its kitchen odor continues to amuse me, as do her blossoms.

Not to be overlooked for the beauty of their flowers in a range of purples, blues, reds, and white are the clematises. Sooner or later one or the other variety will find its

◄ Boston Ivy. *Parthenocissus tricuspidata* as mentioned on p.172.

Cityscape ▲
Thunbergia alata

way into your garden too. But for lack of space I will have to limit myself to some brief observations. It is a family full of temperamental gents and ladies, glamorous when at their peak but requiring attention and some basic knowledge as to which of the three groups they belong to. General Sikorski did well for me for several years, until he lost his final battle to fungus. Chlorotic Madame LeCoultre has been moved around a few times in an attempt to alleviate her condition, naturally after many applications of iron, but hopefully will approve of her next deluxe accommodation: rich loam, good drainage, feet in the shade, head in the sun. Only Perle d'Azur is happy at its first site on the fence of the dog pen, where it adorns the top tier, and where the typical leggy growth of clematises is well placed as it does not interfere with the inmates' view. The distinct drawback of all the clematises is that when they race ahead without the gardener's careful intervention it becomes impossible to sort out the tangled mess high up. The flowers of all climbers can and theoretically want to display themselves in a sheetlike manner, but all too often the young shoots of clematis err around aimlessly and entwine themselves beyond hope, as they are extremely fragile and snap the moment they get touched even by delicate hands. I just removed one of the easiest and freest blooming of all clematises, a "Jackmanii," from high up on an arbor, where every year it formed a chaotic ball of inextricable stems studded with dark blue flowers: a nest of ninnies so to speak. Since I have little to lose, I cut it back to a height of five inches and replanted the rootstock next to a rose rambler at the foot of my healthy pistachio shrub, enabling it to hitch a ride on the many nearby branches. I'll see next summer if perchance it could be coaxed into spreading out in all directions.

So if it is heads or tails whether a climber gives the performance it should, what is the good of having yet one more clematis? Why not gamble and give something truly exotic a try? This I did with two plants that as a matter of course became points of great interest. They are my first stops when I dart out of the house after a severe cold spell to take count of any casualties. To increase its chance to survive winter I put a plastic collar about eight inches high around the base of my pure white, passionflower in the fall, filling it with sand, hoping that should the top die, it might regrow from the root—which it did for three years running before it finally gave up. It was well worth the effort, even if it had been there for just one season. The other prizewinning specimen, which gets the same winter protection, is an *Abutilon megapotamicum*, a lovely rambler producing great quantities of bell-shaped red and yellow flowers that look like pendulous Indian earrings. Not only has it not died but it keeps blooming well into the winter, leaving me to wonder where it gets such resilience and energy from. I've had it for nine years now, and regard it as an undeserved treat.

Blue wisteria at the Alhambra in Spain

Gabrielle Van Zuylen resting up under a canopy
of blue *Thunbergia grandiflora* in Sotogrande.

Timothy Hill

By the time we reached the prime of our lives we had done practically everything a happy couple can do together, except for the one I never thought I would consider: to build a house. That I came around to this foreign idea must be ascribed to my husband's remarkable persuasive powers. He occasionally had flirted with the idea of trading in our delightful semi-rural life in Westchester County north of New York City for the real thing: farmland. To me this seemed purely academic, and it did not occur to me to pay attention to the upcoming attraction, the seven-year itch. Not itching for an extramarital fling, but for moving to some other habitat. For Larry had shown himself to be a Don Giovanni of real estate, and periodically was grabbed by a hot desire for a different apartment or a new house, never mind how contentedly he was ensconced in his current home. Real estate agents were sometimes dropped in on just for kicks, in improbable places, and since nothing ever came of it I considered myself a very lucky woman indeed. But lately the scenario had taken on a tint of urgency, as horseback riding in the suburbs had become severely limited. What ensued could be compared to a very brief game of chess. In a short skirmish between American mobility and a tenacious Swiss attachment to the ground one occupies, I was swayed by the suggestion of adventure combined with the notion that I could have a house and a garden exactly the way I wanted them (as if I did not have them already). Like any savvy art dealer, Larry knew that a good sale is one where the buyer leaves the shop feeling this was his lucky day. That, however, was not a foregone conclusion, for when my Don Giovanni showed me the site he considered, tears welled up in my eyes. And not from joy. What I was looking at was a bare hillside with only one tree in the main view, an old but ailing English oak near a crumbling stone wall halfway down the field. Nor was the woodland in the back a feast for the eyes; it was all secondary growth and accordingly unkempt. An existing, uninhabited small farmhouse, a silo, and some barns close to the entrance near the road made

The ancient oak tree and our house way back

it the gate to heaven for my equestrian husband, since a stable manager and horses could be put up there without further delay. This was the scene between Amenia and Millbrook in Dutchess County, New York State, in 1983. With a strong dose of imagination it was vaguely comparable to the soft hills of Wiltshire in England, minus the climate. Russell Page's laconic summary was: freezing winters and a massive deer problem. Then he asked if we had a body of water, which we did not. So that was that. Nor did the address "Bangall Amenia Road" win me over. I would have much preferred letterheads with "Skunk Misery Lane," where we had looked at a rickety old house too shabby to buy.

Since Larry was familiar with the area and all the available properties from riding, it had not taken him long to find that narrow strip of land, "only" 200 acres, which was wedged between the large estate of the actor James Cagney and the vast expanse of Wethersfield Farm, the philanthropist Chauncey Devereux Stillman's property. Both these gentlemen lived quiet lives, savoring the Arcadian charms of longhorn cattle, horse carriages, comfortable country houses, trails, and cabins in the wood. When we encountered Mr. Stillman on his Sunday outings with four-in-hand and a properly attired groom, it was easy to forget what century we were living in.

Having chosen the land with the intention to build, the site for the house was a given. It was to be discreetly tucked away towards the back of the property, far removed from the road and invisible to neighbors. Buildings dominating from crests and hilltops are in questionable taste except for old ones with a history. To reside on a peak was plausible in the past when such a situation may have had its charm and function, whereas today changes to the silhouette of the horizon are an act of extreme annoyance, not to say aggression. A 360-degree view, moreover, brings the risk that some newcomer will put up an eyesore within your view before you can say Jack Robinson. Paul Heyer, a friend and fine architect with the necessary sensitivity for the wishes of his clients, was happy to undertake the task of designing a contemporary version of our beloved white colonial house in Katonah. He did this very successfully, emphasizing its simplicity by applying a touch of the Shakers' austere esthetic, which during the seventies and eighties had reached the forefront of taste in America for anybody interested in design.

Given American efficiency, the wooden house was erected astonishingly fast. When halfway finished the whole south facade suddenly bulged out as if the structure had decided to become a ship. But the builders just laughed, took a few nails, and simply hammered the whole side back. Lots of insulation was inserted between the outer and inner walls. This was in the 1980s when America had woken up to the necessity of saving fuel, whereas at the Old Apple Farm in Katonah, built in 1928, no insulation of any kind could be found. By contrast, in the old part of Zurich, in a nineteenth-century apartment building where we lived for a while, straw mixed with hundred-year-old dung poured out from behind a wall when it was opened for a minor structural change in 1996.

▲ Sunday outing

Contour farming, corn alternating with alfalfa.

An island of *Hydrangea paniculata* "Grandiflora"

No time was lost preparing for the trees we urgently needed at Timothy Hill, as we named our new place after the grass that was growing in the fields. We had a small lot behind the farmhouse dug up as a temporary nursery for whatever shrubs and young trees we were going to pick up along the way, even before building began. A hilarious memory of that makeshift patch was a single Mother Hubbard squash I planted in an unoccupied zone so as not to let the prepared ground go to waste. It developed at a galloping speed, several inches a day and one could have sworn to see it happening. At the end of the summer it presented us with an impressive bluish gray monster the size of a young piglet, which we kept as a curiosity and never ate. Annuals surely grow faster than trees, which is why vegetable gardens with their quick rewards are so popular.

My personal garden in the foreground with view of the striped hillside.

Once the shell of the house was standing, we set out to choose some sizable trees. We found them at Rosedale, that excellent nursery on the Saw Mill River Parkway, and at Halka, another nursery in New Jersey which specialized in specimens that had already some years on their back. Assuring hardiness is a must when you buy trees. Although a good nursery gives a guarantee for a replacement in case of a negative outcome—and they won't sell you plants not fit for your zone—the offer is only for the individual tree you buy and not for the transport or the cost of the work. Moreover, we had entered a stage of life where lost time began to look worse than the loss of a small sum of money. If restrictions imposed by climatic conditions seem regrettable at first, I have learned that limitations can work as a challenge and a positive force. America's colder zones have amazing riches of hardy plants. To create shade near the porch, two fairly large sugar maples were a must. Other maples and poplars were added to break up the view on the large expanses of grassland surrounding us. The presence even of only medium-sized trees helps to gage the distance which in an empty field remains uncertain. I am almost tempted to say that a tree planted within an empty space makes its borders seem further away.

The defined area behind the house between the main entrance and the edge of the woods was easier to design than the wide-open landscape everywhere else. Giving in to an impulse, we acquired a young katsura tree with graceful, heart-shaped leaves. It had an enchanting surprise up its sleeve. A couple of years later when walking to the house from the garage I suddenly found myself engulfed by a strong scent of burnt sugar that had me wonder who on earth was in the kitchen making jam. But no such action was going on. It was the autumnal fragrance of the katsura leaves. Of course, we also planted many smaller specimens such as apple and crab apple trees; they are as indispensable as the peons in a chess set. Three young *Liquidambar styraciflua*, slightly risky because not dependably hardy in our zone, proved irresistible and were ordered with apprehension, mitigated by our rather frequent so-what-the-heck attitude. And a *Stewartia* of some kind that I had gotten from a catalog house unexpectedly became a feather in my cap. It resembled camellias but with sweet smelling blossoms, and in the middle of summer to boot, when few trees come up with a special performance. Six small-leaved linden trees were an absolute necessity to hide the hideous, gigantic TV radar dish at the edge of the woods. However, none of this amounted to what one could seriously call the bones of the garden. Our property was simply too large. And all we really wanted was a pleasant landscape, neither belabored nor manicured but just well kept.

What needed immediate attention was the brand-new house, which looked as if a good gust of wind could simply blow it away. Foundation plantings had to anchor it more visibly to the ground. By that time I had acquired enough practical knowledge and some addresses where good material could be found. In horticultural terms, our area near Millbrook was, unlike Westchester, which catered to a more sophisticated public, still the hinterland. The big new wave of green passion had not reached it yet, and local resources like the agricultural extension program had only meager stock, such as those detestable six-packs of snapdragons and pansies that paid no regard to their colors. The Internet did not exist yet. The majority of today's shoppers cannot possibly imagine what life was like back then in the 1980s, and what detours and determination it took to find the item one was looking for, whether for the garden or otherwise. But thanks to the offerings of some well-furnished and specialized catalog houses, to plan and plant the foundation borders of the white clapboard house became a real pleasure. There was one on each side of the house offering spots for every appetite: full sun, partial shade, full shade, and every variation in between. In my newest find, the catalog for Klehm's Nursery in Champain, Illinois, I found all the peonies one could dream of, and stuffed the western border of the brand-new building with as many of the spectacular bronze- and apricot-colored tree peonies as I could fit in, with *Kirengeshoma palmata* and *Tiarella cordifolia* for company. For the climbing *Lonicera halliana* on the wall behind them we had trellises made, the tops of which were attached to the wall with little chains so that the mature plants could remain in place, leaning forward whenever the repainting of the house became necessary. Equally successful was the scheme on the north side near the main entrance. The European cranberry bush, *Viburnum opulus*, took off splendidly, happily sharing the ground with huge hostas and different ferns. A bed of old-fashioned roses was placed beneath the windows of the two guest rooms for maximum admiration. To flesh out the rest we had to add shrubs. If my acquisitive impulses for buying plants were restrained in the past, I now went whole hog. No more timid purchases. Nothing less than three, five, seven, or more would do to colonialize what at that point were still fairly bleak surroundings. For clumps out in the open to have something to look at, the old standbys forsythia, lilacs, and deutzias did yeoman's duty and were easy to come by. Groupings of larger shrubs, either six or more of the same kind, henceforth were nicknamed our *Îles-de-France*. Repeating that method later in Italy they became *Isolottos*. For the finishing touch near the garage, prickly berberis was chosen for an impenetrable hedge that earned its keep in the fall with bright red orange leaves.

But there was a much less common shrub I aimed for, hoping to introduce it to our zone as a pioneer. Hazelnuts. In Europe they are commonplace and planted for crops of filberts. For the longest time I could not find any, until one day I leafed through the catalog of a nursery not far from Buffalo, New York, and my heart made a jump. It listed what I was looking for, in a town with the melodious name Canandaigua, which I rolled off my tongue aloud like a mantra, savoring every vowel and recalling the illustrations of my childhood books showing the people we affectionately called Red Indians picking nuts. The ten young shrubs I received by mail found their destination near our swimming pool, further away from the house, and they flourished and fruited, but I do not know for how long since we did not stay in Amenia forever, as I had thought we would.

The peony border

My plot barely finished

Satisfying as these involvements were, my hottest wish from day one had been a flower garden of my own. The moment the house was staked out I began to concentrate on where exactly this special haven should be. I was sure of one thing: that it had to beckon from a certain distance, making its presence felt in an impressionistic manner without showing details too clearly. I had to be prevented from jumping up the moment I noticed a weed or saw something that needed fixing. Benign neglect had to take priority over the obsessive nature-controlling urges we gardeners are prone to. The garden of my dreams is actually an enclosed space, surrounded by ancient walls where protection from deer, rabbits, excessively high winds, and other disturbances is pretty much guaranteed. But no such space even vaguely suggested itself, and the handsome old walls were far away across the ocean. Instead, I was looking at large swatches of empty pasture, rolling softly from north to south. The descent running from east to west on the hillside was somewhat steeper and dipped down near the bottom to a large tract of wetland that was home to moisture-loving native trees and shrubs. From there the terrain rose again on the opposite side of the valley, where it presented its cultivated surface in a pattern of broad horizontal stripes in alternating colors. It was this most attractive view on modern agriculture that had caught my eye right off the bat when we bought the property.

An aerial view, looking south, ▶
onto the crosswalk with arches.

So I set out from the southeast corner of the future house and walked some seventy steps diagonally uphill into the empty field. When I turned around I saw that everything fell nicely into place. Looking straight at the contour-farmed hillside opposite, I was very pleased with this elegant background. The geometric neatness of the agricultural pattern made me decide on a rectangular shape for my garden, with its main axis running from east to west, that is to say perpendicular to the stripes in my distant view. Thus my vantage point—the spot where I was going to sit at the end of the day to moon over what nature and I had accomplished—was at the center of the upper border of my chosen patch of land, from where my eyes could comfortably drift over the garden in the foreground and continue gloriously into the golden sunset. The perfect plot.

I had a 16 by 20-meter rectangle plowed up, with added peat moss and some horse manure so as to get a head start. A year after it had its chance to mature, the activity began for real. No amateurish soil tests here: we sent properly collected samples to the agricultural extension program to be analyzed. They turned out to be fairly similar to the ones in Katonah, and since the pH value was roughly the same as before, things looked propitious. I had learned the basics and was ready to plow full steam ahead. I had the plot edged with timber, four-by-fours this time rather than the railway ties of the past, which in the meantime were found to poison the soil nearby. Next I established two main walkways, dividing the rectangle descending down from east to west, and a cross axis running north to south, where the terrain was not on an incline but flat. They were covered in bluestone, resting on a bed of sand. Intent on creating outside borders, I had a post-and-rail fence put up one meter in from the edge, going all around, leaving four open sections for the paths. The fence worked out handsomely, providing a support for future ramblers or a place to lean against. It also turned out to be an excellent device to give a sense of proportion and scale. I didn't need a measuring stick any more, but could take my clues from the height of the posts and the distance between them. An apple tree punctuated each corner inside the fence. They fairly soon made crowns big enough to cast a little shade, helping some plants such as lettuces to stay a tad cooler. Millbrook and Amenia, being inland, often have sweltering heat in summer, so even just a suggestion of shade was welcome. Some additions were made later, notably cinderblocks to enforce the timber edges and protect them from damage by mowing machines. A platform at the upper end to place both a bench and a large trunk to store tools in was an equally practical idea, as I could leave the wooden furniture exposed to the elements all year long. The last items were four arches that a smith made to order, which I could not resist painting in that inimitable bluish

◀ Irises, oriental poppies, and geraniums

Looking from the heart of my flower garden towards the house.

green with a nod to Monet. The grapes that grew on them were something of an excuse to get that pergola effect, the climate of upstate New York not lending itself to the vast possibilities of Italy or France.

The outside borders, one on each side, all in full sun, permitted me to elaborate on four different flower schemes. The peony border was planted rapidly, as I had brought along my favorite ones from Katonah. Their often-lamented brief booming period is easily countenanced by their magnificent display and intense perfume, and above all by their longevity. They will be there for generations to come. Nor do they require a lot of work as long as the staking is done early, something that is easiest to achieve with prefabricated hoops. For their companionship I added a handful of *Dictamnus rubra*, their sturdy pink spires mingling to perfection with the huge balls of the peonies, and then continuing to bloom much much longer. Apparently they are very long lived, too, and you can try to set a match to them to justify their common name "gas plant." Need I say it? That never worked for me.

For the border on the opposite side I planned a second act for an early summer parade of oriental poppies, lupines, irises, various geraniums, and penstemons on a luxurious backdrop of rich blue *Baptisia australis*. Let the photographs speak for themselves. The lowest border, visible from the table on our porch, was given over to midsummer flowers chosen for an overall painterly effect. Globe thistles, helichrysums, yarrows, phlox, clouds of perovskias, and similar stuff turned out

Oriental poppies galore,
irises, geraniums,
columbines

Baptisia australis, lupines

The summer border

The fun border, drumstick
onions, borage etc.

well, equipped to withstand the blazing summer heat. The uppermost long bed near the bench was to house all the material I had not decided yet where to plant: wrong shipments from catalog houses, gifts from well-meaning friends, extras from other people's gardens, thoughtless purchases, and surpluses of invasive plants. It turned out be full of fun. He who has no expectations cannot be disappointed. A memorable moment still echoing in my head is the belly laugh I got from Richard Diebenkorn when I mentioned the name horehound for the inconspicuous herb he was looking at inquiringly. He loved dogs, retained a schoolboy's delight in basic jokes, and thought the name was spelled with an initial "w." The herbs I actually used in the kitchen got their separate patch near the porch, and their names our friend would undoubtedly have heard before.

More of this happy-go-lucky approach went on in the four quarters inside the fence. I subdivided each of them into nine small plots. The narrow paths forming the grid were not paved but simply left as trampled soil. In this manner the earth in each small plot was never walked on but remained soft and friable, which is in part why my explorative plantings were so successful. Among them were studies of color combinations, plant associations, coinciding blooming periods, new varieties of flowers, and other experiments my curiosity kept me busy with.

Among the typical pleasures of country houses are the manifold little changes and improvements we fantasize about, adding something or other at leisurely intervals. For us it was an ongoing process, the teamwork of two likeminded temperaments, taking delight in the slow process. In this fashion we happily sailed from one year to the next. On the evening of October 3, 1987, we went to bed with all the trees and shrubs still in their full mantle of green leaves. The spectacle of New England autumn colors was to spread through our region and down to New York City in about two weeks as it always did. When we woke up next morning, the light squeezing in through those inevitable gaps between the roller shades and window frames seemed unusually bright. Hearing muffled gunshots, we figured that there had to be some hunters around. But the shots followed each other faster and faster, as if we were in the middle of a war. When we opened the shades we gasped, stunned by the unbearable whiteness of what we saw. Huge snowflakes came hurtling down in massive quantities, inexorably adding inches and inches to the already thick blanket of snow. The gunshots we had heard weren't gunshots at all. They were the sounds of tree branches breaking under the weight of the wet snow that had found support on their green leaves. Thousands of branches broke off with a loud crack, or sometimes with a groaning moan. Many trees were split in half. The storm lasted for hours. Aside from some minor earthquakes and occasional floods, I had never witnessed a natural disaster. Nature had bared her teeth and left us in a state of shock. It was an early sign that the seasons were out of whack, and also demonstrated why deciduous plants must let go of their leaves before the snow arrives. When stepping outside once the snowfall had stopped, we hardly recognized where we were. All the trees' branches without exception were bent down steeply. Most shrubs were no longer visible but had spread out on the ground in a circle, looking like starfish under the thick white cover. It was hard to believe that this was the same place we had seen yesterday. The soundtrack did not cease for many more hours, even after the snowfall let up. We remained without electricity for six days and were officially called a disaster zone. The woods and the whole region were devastated and did not recover for many years. By sheer luck our place had less damage than many neighboring properties on account of our plantings still being in their early youth. Evidently, children roll better with the punches than older folks.

That disaster notwithstanding, not just my garden but the whole adventure was heaven on earth, all seven years of it. But as we know, no paradise lasts forever, and the end of Timothy Hill slowly came into focus until the writing was unmistakably on the wall, because the glowing embers in my Don Giovanni's chest had flared up yet again and made us move once more. And this time it brought us much further away, taking a big leap over the ocean to the heart of Europe.

The harvest, including red and green hazelnuts

A Thorny Issue

T he rose is a creature that defies language. Even Gertrude Stein ran out of words pretty fast. Wine and perfume face parallel problems, as they too possess iconic power and belong to large clans that appeal to our senses. However hard experts try to describe those substances, they fall short of evoking the precise sensation their seductive ingredients produce to eyes, nose, palate, and brain. And it is useless to bring in the proverbial twenty-five words Eskimos have for snow. If THEY were faced with the 3,000 varieties of roses now in cultivation they would struggle too. The best we can do is describe them, codify them, create categories that have characteristics or origins in common, and rhapsodize. But the actual experience can only come from having a rose in front of our eyes and burying our nose in its ravishing center, "in real time" as they call it today.

No flower has been subjected more to the tides of fashion than the rose, from its earliest appearance until today. Its career began around the Mediterranean basin in antiquity, when it was a symbol for love and beauty among the Greeks, and later grown by the Romans as a crop, yielding the fragrant petals needed in vast amounts for the decoration of their premises. But equally baffling to us is that the plant as a whole was passed over and had to wait for a botanical description until much later. When Christianity joined the game and ultimately managed to intertwine the rose's pagan aspect with its own rites—as it did with many heathen feasts and customs—the flower was turned into a central symbol, as in the rosary for instance, or when white for the Virgin Mary and red for the blood of Christ. The secular Middle Ages used it in stylized form as an emblem and generously sprinkled it onto coats of arms or depicted it in illuminated books. Madonnas in their little paradise or "rose gardens" and the "War of the Roses" are two examples among many. Indicative of that era

The high hedge of Albertine roses ▶
forming a circle was the beginning of a
rose garden in the hills near Piacenza.

Dorothy Perkins, a docile and exceptionally floriferous rambler

was that most flowers were depicted on a gold background rather than in a natural setting. Every epoch has its own approach to nature—and apparently to roses too.

For many centuries the cherished old roses—blooming profusely but only once in early summer—trotted along in horticulture, with romantic labels like damasks, centifolias, gallicas, albas, and musks. They all filled lords and ladies and poets with delight, and some hybridization of these fairly hardy and disease-resistant shrubs was undertaken, though on a modest scale compared to what was to follow. Beyond the pleasure of their blooms, these old fashioneds offer us an amusement we can freely indulge in: name dropping. Should you be a sucker for lineages and pedigrees you need not look further but supply your garden with "Duc de Guiche," "Duchesse d'Angoulême," "Comte de Chambord," "Koenigin von Dänemark," "Cardinal de Richelieu," and so on. The best-known patron of roses was Empress Josephine, who, as a serious botanist and collector, meddled in politics to have blockades lifted for her botanical imports, which shows to what degree Napoleon was besotted with her. Of course, there exists an "Empress Josephine," with a "Souvenir de la Malmaison" in tow. Plant a "Chapeau de Napoléon" next to them and you begin to feel that you are rubbing shoulders with the highest level of society.

Towards the end of the eighteenth century, a sea change burst onto the scene when four different China tea roses were brought to Europe, just in time for Empress Josephine to get her hands on one of them. New imports never fail to create a sensation, but the stunning fact of the Chinese rose's ability to produce blooms continuously propelled roses in general to the apex of horticultural desires and made hybridization explode. The rose was soon named the queen of flowers. It has a lot to recommend itself as its looks change daily, from the opening of its bud to the unfurling of its petals, depending on the variety, from the simplicity of only five in the dog rose, for instance, to twenty and so through to over a hundred in a centifolia. Its life has many acts: promising, fulfilling, regretfully ageing, and then expiring like a soprano on stage. On no two days does the blossom of a rose look the same, and neither do its tints, which change with age and are subject to the rise and fall of the temperature, subtly sometimes, more pronounced in others. "Lavender Pinocchio," for one, takes the cake as its colors bounce around like in a litmus test, reaching its zenith when brisker days arrive. Compare the rose's performance to

Tessa Traeger in London's Battersea Park shakes off spent blossoms preparing the rose shrub for a photograph.

that of a tithonia for instance, that retains its bright orange blossom and velvety stiff self to its very end. It has its charm too, but I would not call it versatile. As an aside I should add that cool weather and overcast skies intensify the colors of all flowers, which may be the reason why Scottish ladies are renowned flower gardeners. Later in the season when roses have finished producing blossoms they compensate for their absence with many differently shaped but always vivid red hips, which liven up the grey and foggy days.

Above all, the rose stands out for its varied spatial application: as a rambler, climber, small standard, groundcover, or bedding plant. This assures it of its place as the most popular but also the most indiscriminately planted of all flowers. Roses can be trained in all directions and are paragons for vertical accents, on special supports like wooden pyramids or towers, or draped like garlands on wires or chains. Their fantastic display when they spread themselves over cupolas and gazebos or cover whole walls with literally hundreds of buds ready to burst into blooms is unsurpassable. It is as easy to like roses as it is to like Mozart's music. Other plants and composers take longer to appreciate. To the discerning gardener, however, the naked truth is that they are difficult plants. When grown outside their native climate—part of their ancestry is tropical—they are vulnerable to diseases and other malaises. And, truth be told, most roses are an unattractive sight when not in bloom. They clamor for a garden of their own, where they can hide out when looking their worst, that is to say for the bigger part of the year. If you are an incurable rose addict, a separate rose garden is a distinct possibility should the space allow for it. Here too Empress Josephine was a pioneer: she made the very first garden exclusively for growing roses at her Château de Malmaison.

The divide between "old" and "modern" roses was established at the turn of the nineteenth century, when the new tea roses and floribundas were in full swing. They hogged the center of the stage for half a century but then enthusiasm began to flag, which enabled the old-fashioned roses to be invited back by a new gardening public that had become disenchanted with the increasingly stereotypical look and often lacking fragrance of the teas and floribundas. Luckily, David Austin under the aegis of Graham Stuart Davies came along and bred the perfume back into them as well as reinstating their true identity as shrubs. In due course they became known as "English Roses." In that form they can be successfully mixed in with other flowers and shrubs in a border, or used in naturalized settings even next to the likes of olive trees. They currently are among the top favorites and new varieties are still being bred and scooped up by many of us.

◄◄ Federico Forquet's pergola dressed up in May Queen roses.

Tour de Malakoff

Sissinghurst's rose garden

Speaking for myself, I became partial to old roses not on account of any romantic idea or fashion but because they withstood the cold of our American winters and finished their single blooming cycle before the Japanese beetles arrived. After some initial hesitation when taking my first gardening steps in Katonah, I had also bought a really juicy modern "Whisky Mac." I allowed myself that extravaganza only after I had found the right place for it, a boudoir of his own as it were, where Mac's bright tangerine shade did not conflict with the other colors nearby. As usual, location and the company we keep is what counts. When gardening in Italy twenty years later and suddenly discovering that roses do well in clay soil, I naturally veered towards the David Austins. They are richly perfumed and beautiful, but oh can they sting. While thorns differ widely among the many varieties—"Zéphirine Drouhin" for instance is almost thorn-free—the Austin roses have them in aggressive abundance which makes them particularly difficult to use in flower arrangements. Nonetheless, when we are in the hands of a new infatuation we tend to overlook such drawbacks. As La Rochefoucauld put it 200 years ago: on pardonne tant que l'on aime.

Rosarians are highbrow gardeners who can sometimes be recognized by the armor they wear, in the form of leather gloves which reach almost up to their shoulders to protect themselves from the nasty scratches roses can cause. As a greenhorn I had an interesting encounter with such a specialist, finding myself engaged in a conversation with the rosarian of Brooklyn Botanical Garden, standing on the terrace gazing at the vast expanse of blazing blossoms down below. This man, whose name my brain has not retained, was far from overawed by the spectacle but seemed to be looking down onto the sea of roses, not just physically but figuratively as well. After a few introductory words he revealed that there was only a handful of specimens he allowed into his private sphere of praiseworthiness. "Self-cleaning" was the unendearing word he came up with; I had hitherto known it only in connection with kitchen appliances. And when he included the rather banal "Iceberg" among the roses that met his standards, my heart sank, as I associated the name with that coarse head of lettuce residing for weeks and weeks in American refrigerator drawers. I left the BBG that day somewhat disillusioned. But as the years go by, having been indoctrinated by an expert, I pay increased attention to how roses age and how they shed their spent petals. Those rose shrubs I can free of their wilted blossoms with the light tap of a bamboo stick or a sharp jet of water are definitely preferable to the ones that obstinately cling to the unsightly brown balls their former splendors have turned into. My final reconciliation with "Iceberg" was mediated by discovering its European name, "Schneewittchen." It currently grows in a difficult, half-shady corner near the garage, where its impeccable whiteness looks refreshing and cheers me up in every phase of its cycle, letting go of its petals in the lightest breeze. Thus I have come to regard ageing gracefully as a valuable asset, and even make special efforts to apply that concept to myself.

"Amy Robsart" has a few petals
while "Charles de Mills" comes up
with close to a hundred.

Idyllic scene near Lake Zurich: an Indian bean
tree lending support to a "Kiftsgate" climbing rose.

A dreamy combination of honeysuckle and an English rose

West of Eden

W̶e should award a blue ribbon to Eve in the garden of Eden, for she saw that the forbidden tree was good for food and pleasant to the eyes, and that it was a tree to make one wise. She clearly was the first dendrologist. Whoever wrote that paragraph in the Bible bestowing special status on a tree and linking it to the concept of knowledge put his finger on a great wisdom. Learning increases appreciation in all things, but when it comes to trees, knowledge is of the essence if we want to benefit from the riches of their gifts and pay them a little respect. Begin by acquiring their names for instance. Dendrology, the study of trees, invites us to sharpen our powers of observation and in the process memorize a new vocabulary. We learn to identify a species by the shape of the whole tree or by parts of it, by its leaves, fruits, and flowers, or by the texture of its bark, or by the crown and the way it ramifies. Even its root system, though hidden in the ground, has a recognizable blueprint. The pundits have it that there are connoisseurs and sylvanomaniacs among us who can recognize some trees by the sound of their branches in the breeze, or by the shadow pattern they cast on the ground. Would that I could.

It is impossible to overrate the role of trees. Without them there would be no fire, no fuel, no smelting of metals, no tools or tool handles, no furnishings from floorboards to rafters, no wheels, vehicles, or ships, and therefore no large-scale transport or trade—in short there would be no civilization as we know it. And probably no humans either, because we supposedly came down from the trees where we learned to use our hands like monkeys. Not that the list of the bounty we receive from the arboreal world is finished here. Beyond timber we get fibers, resins, gums, food, medicinal substances, and more, but maybe above all else there is the shade they dispense, the humidity they store, and the habitat they provide for others. In the tropics, single trees are known to host thousands of different animals and organisms.

◄ Eve's choice

A palm grove near Zagora, Morocco

It would be hard to find a culture or a tribe that does not revere trees in some form or other. Ancient trees strike us as noble. They are individuals that have been around for much longer than we have, and they are likely to outlive us as well. Silent eyewitnesses to history, they sometimes have a story to tell; a cross section revealing their annual rings is like a memory card that stores information. The slice of the redwood at the American Museum of Natural History in New York City, communicating its timetable measured in millennia and dwarfing our concept of time, is a striking example of such a record. It demonstrates how puny our human existence is when compared to the lifespan of a sequoia. The marker on that huge cross section pinpointing the year when Columbus discovered America shows that the sequoia was already 900 years old at that moment. It is an object lesson that dispenses an altered sense of history.

Our habit of applying hierarchal thinking to trees is somewhat arbitrary. It puts hardwoods at the top, heavy in weight, and when set afire burning for a long time, emitting high temperatures. That essential quality must already have been evident to our forebears of the Bronze and Iron Ages. It remained a burning issue, so to speak, right through the millennia, having its impact on industry and affecting many lesser aspects of daily life. In the days before electric ranges, the cook's expertise in which logs to pick was part of her craft, as this was the way to regulate the heat under the pots. Young boys, on the other hand, who were not interested in cooking up a stew but intent on building model airplanes, turned to the opposite end of the spectrum for South American balsa wood, which is light as a feather and can be cut with a knife. There are legions of trees about which most of us know little or nothing at all. And yet they have been discovered as the perfect source of a multitude of specialized objects: billiard balls, violin bows, umbrella handles, and piano keys, without which our lives would be less refined and much less fun. The exploitation of forests therefore started early and was already rampant in the past. But the scope of what we face today—the annihilation of rainforests and the increasing number of apocalyptic wild fires—is unprecedented. The tragic

Conifers and deciduous trees in Central Park, New York

disappearance of large wooded areas affects the weather patterns of the whole planet. Reforestation is a laborious process and not always successful. Responsible parents and governments should plant three saplings for each child born and see them to maturity. These would not only help to produce more oxygen for immediate consumption but also provide long-term storage for some of the CO_2 the exploding population will have to deal with.

Far-flung places have cast their spell on botanists since history began. Tropical zones in particular have lured explorers and adventurers into virgin territory, dangling visions of fortunes made from precious woods or spices in front of their eyes and noses. Mysterious jungles and exotic riches send us dreaming, but when returning to the reality of our daily lives we find ourselves drawing tighter and tighter circles around hearth and home. In the smaller world of gardens, other criteria apply than in the wild and we reshuffle the cards. The first thing we do is to rule out trees that grow to huge dimensions. Unless we own a lot of land, beeches, redwoods, cedars of Lebanon, and other potential giants are better off in public parks, those tranquil islands of green shade within the fabric of human settlements. Or we relegate them to arboretums and botanical gardens. In these outdoor schoolrooms we are bound to make new friends. They are certainly worth visiting, for they enable us to study the plants in all seasons and help us make informed choices about what we would like to adorn our front yard with. How often have such outings given me the impulse to search in garden centers for just that shade of brick red I had spotted on a labeled buckeye, or find the persimmon named "Vanilla" that poses as a sort of Christmas tree for us when festooned with dozens and dozens of big round orange fruit in December—most delightfully so when an unexpected snowfall turned our Italian scenery white.

Many considerations must go into what trees we choose to plant. It would be foolish to take risks with subjects that are unsuitable for our specific location and later see them decimated because we had not reckoned with the vicissitudes of the climate in an atypical year. Plummeting mercury, biblical droughts, changed wind patterns roll around with increased frequency now that climate stability has left us. Let's do our homework first and read up what a tree's requirements are. Some detest having their feet in water and need good drainage. Others should be positioned away from wind because of the brittleness of their branches. By far the most com-

Serious tree planting requires a tractor and four men.

mon mistake, however, is to plant trees too close together. Nothing is as hard to visualize as the shape of a mature individual when for the time being we are dealing with a mere sapling, selecting a spot and driving a suggestive broom upside down into the ground. It is an absolute necessity to calculate what the ultimate height and width of a tree will be before we choose its precise position. We also have to stick to the distance between trees prescribed, tape measure in hand. For it is truly disheartening to have planted some trees randomly and then see them crowd out each other after just a few years. At that point, sacrificing one or some of them is the only remedy since it will be too late to separate their roots, which have hopelessly grown into each other. There can be no fooling around either when it comes to the restraints imposed by climate and soil. If you really must have a fling with a flamboyant subtropical in upstate New York, reserve such a folly for an herbaceous perennial and call it a passing fancy.

Planting a tree is as serious a matter as getting married. It is from my husband that I first learned about the possibility of transplanting trees, and big ones at that. Up to then I had taken trees for granted and assumed they grew wherever their seeds had sprouted or maybe where a professional gardener had carefully put a small whip into a well-prepared hole in the ground. The notion of going on a shopping spree to a nursery and choosing nearly full-grown conifers, linden, horse chestnuts, and such to be delivered to us when dormant amazed me. Yet my husband's efficiency, his lack of patience, and craving for immediate satisfaction predisposed him to such actions and soon had me nickname him Luigi Quattordici (Louis XIV). For the latter was not given to dillydallying either, and sometimes had whole boskets replanted overnight to surprise his subjects in the morning. Fittingly, it is in France that my mate had acquired his arboreal passion. When settling in Paris as a young man and opening an art gallery in the rue du Dragon, he enthusiastically immersed himself in the culture of his newly adopted country and remained a Francophile to the end of his days. The attention the French government pays to trees is one of its incontestable glories. Paris has the best kept parks ever, and hundreds of village squares from Normandy to Provence boast splendid examples of clipped hornbeams, pleached limes, pollarded plane trees, and more, proudly showing off the Gallic spirit of formal landscaping. Even in their former colonies, the French lined the streets they found with native trees to form the allées that reminded them

Ready for transplanting

Tree surgeon

of home. Some of these have survived and are locally still known as "the French Street." An equally grandiose attitude becomes apparent when parks or roadsides in France need to be refurbished, for where a few old or sick trees have to be felled they are not simply replaced by young ones. Often a whole row is cut down and replanted in its entirety.

Transplanting not-so-young trees is indeed possible, but it does not always meet with success. When one of our ancient apple trees in Katonah keeled over in a storm, we had a local nurseryman replace it the following winter with a pink dogwood. Admiring his subject after the deed was done, he assured us that it was doing fine and "doesn't even know it has been transplanted." He sure was right. The tree was dead and never regained consciousness. Things can go wrong when we try to override nature. We've been told, for instance, that anything grown in a pot can be planted out any time, provided we follow up with ample watering. But that is only the theory and not the whole truth. Plants that have been confined for too long may send their roots round and round in their container. And should you have the dumb idea to just pull it out of its plastic pot and sink it into the ground, you are in for an evil surprise because the roots will continue to grow in that spiral fashion, eventually depriving the tree of nourishment by strangling itself. It is therefore necessary to carefully disentangle the roots when planting and make them point outward in every direction. The advantage of an undisturbed root ball thus is partially lost, and with it some of the time we thought we had gained. So maybe it is better after all to choose a younger plant that has not acquired any bad habits. Should you opt for a larger tree that has been growing in the soil in a nursery for several years, avoid selecting a specimen that grows in the middle of a row. It will have sparse growth on the two sides where it was shaded by its neighbors, a defect that will become very visible once it is removed

from its protected spot. Don't listen to the seller who will emphatically assure you that it will fill out in due time. It might not. Inquire if its roots have been properly prepared all along: Trees grown for transplanting have to have incisions made in a circle around their roots every year, so that when the time comes to move them they can be lifted out of the ground unharmed, to then be balled and burlapped. Getting a large tree to its final location is another practical problem as transport may be difficult and, if we are talking about a really large specimen, the spot you pick has to be

Dogwood blossom about to pop open.

Crabapple tree in Connecticut, U.S.A. ▶

Informal horse chestnuts in a Normandy garden

accessible for big machinery and therefore cannot be on a steep slope. Finally, when the moment has come to place the root ball into the prepared hole, don't be tempted to position it a little below ground level, imagining that it will collect more water that way. Humidity around the base of a tree invites disease. The tree must be planted slightly above ground so that drainage is assured. To facilitate proper watering during the first year you can create a circular five-inch-high mud barrier about 50 inches from the trunk. That is the first half of the transplant process. It could be compared to surgery on the human body. Thereafter the recovery of the patient/tree will depend on the intensive aftercare we are prepared to provide.

Just like shrubs, trees come in three different sizes and their final dimension will determine how and where exactly they should be positioned. If you plan to have an array of trees, you may want to tier them so that they rise in height toward the back. Think of the garden as a stage set. It is a good idea to determine your principal point of view—your seat in the audience as it were. It is not necessarily first row in the middle; you may prefer the sight from the corner bedroom on the second floor. But wherever your vantage point, the planting has to look right seen from other angles too.

During my first years in the States, spring struck me as disappointingly short when compared to that dreamy, endlessly blooming season of my youth. But I soon saw that its brief duration is largely compensated for by the magnificence of its autumn, particularly in the northeast. Dry air, warm days, cool nights, and sudden frosts are the basic recipe for autumn colors to arrive overnight and make trees appear as if someone had poured a bucket of paint over their tops, seizing the whole crown in the days thereafter. Due to the sudden retreat of the chlorophyll in the leaves, that picturesque spectacle offers reds, maroons, purplish blacks, and yellows that nearly put the color of flowers to shame. In Europe, by contrast, the rains and fogs of autumn largely produce a muted palette of rusts and pale gold, suggestive of melancholic poems perhaps, but certainly lacking the explosive exuberance of the American fall. As I soon learnt, some of the best colors are produced by sugar maples, red oaks, red maples, American ash, gum trees, dogwoods, and witch hazels, that is to say indigenous American trees. Thus it did not take me long to suggest to my friends they should consider spending their budget on autumn plantings rather than on spring displays.

A formal walk between sugar maples and sculptures at Wethersfield Estate in the Hudson Valley, U.S.A.

Since an ardent desire for novelty is lodged at the core of human nature, plants from elsewhere have whetted our appetite since forever. The importation of trees started as early as that of textiles, decorative glass, and glittery trinkets, although they are not quite the same as objects for they come with the risk that a coveted rare find from another region may dislike its new place and perish. Facing defeat is part of the gardening game, somewhat easier to take with small plants than with trees. But let me point out here that our personal Waterloos are minimal compared to the tragic fates, superhuman efforts, perilous experiences, frequent and heartbreaking losses of arduously collected plant specimens, seeds, records, and valuable notes, in shipwrecks, fires, and other terrifying accidents that the many botanists and plant hunters faced during their expeditions to increase our wealth of plants. From among the long list of explorers and traders I would like to mention John Bartram, the American farmer turned field botanist who, with draper and merchant Peter Collinson in London as his intermediary, became an early exporter of native American seeds and plants, which in turn helped to set off a passion for tree collecting in England. It is sort of a nice twist that an American was instrumental in laying the foundation for Britain taking the lead in horticulture and turning gardening into its national pastime.

There are three European trees that have a larger-than-life quality to them: the oak, the linden, and the yew. Their longevity and economic value account in large part for their status, but they have also earned themselves a star inside the garden. Nobody will be the least bit surprised that my list begins with the oak: the common English oak or *Quercus robur*. Often referred to as the king of the woods, an icon of masculinity and strength, we easily recognize its broad trunk, large crown, horizontal branches, and pretty lobed leaves that remain on the tree well into winter. The width of an ageing oak will eventually become larger than its height, giving it the look of a rugged old warrior. Notwithstanding its endowment of symbolism, the oak was a utilitarian tree in Europe. Oaks were cut down in vast numbers for building ships, both in war and peace. England could never have become the colonial power it was without them. But in a humbler and surprising way these trees were actually grown for food, because their acorns ranked as a big item for feeding pigs. Until well after the Middle Ages, the value of a piece of woodland was calculated on the basis of how many pigs it could feed. Illuminated medieval manuscripts, often illustrating the seasons, are likely to depict swine being shepherded into the woods in November, as can be seen in the exquisite *Les Très Riches Heures du duc de Berry*.

I only got round to planting oaks during the last third of my life, when I learned that contrary to popular myth the common oak did not have a taproot that makes transplanting a lost cause: it is the pin oak that has this dreaded root formation. The ten *Quercus petraea* we planted in Italy are doing well so far and live up to their reputation of being fairly drought resistant; thus our only regret is not having planted more of them sooner. Another valuable addition to our Italian garden is the evergreen *Quercus ilex* or holm oak that is closely associated with classical Italian gardens and southern climes, where it is planted for its remarkably dense shade. It has turned out to be hardier than expected. Once it gets plenty of water it is also much faster growing than the books have us believe. Its thick head of small-leafed foliage not only benefits from but practically demands frequent haircuts. Sitting underneath a *lecce*—its Italian common name—makes me feel quintessentially Italian. These evergreen oaks take up quite a bit of room, and you will find it difficult to grow anything underneath: their mission is to provide that dark, cool shade which is high up on the list of commodities in a country that excels at enjoyment and leisure. I daresay it is well deserved after slugging away for many seasons to make such plants grow.

A sturdy oak after an icestorm

The linden or lime tree, which is often paired with the oak (as in Philemon and Baucis), has quite a different resumé. The *Tilia europaea* is a very feminine tree with large, soft, heart-shaped leaves and strongly scented blossoms, from which an effective fever-reducing infusion is still made today. Its fine-grained wood was favored by medieval artists for their carved sculptures of Madonnas and other saints and therefore came to be named *Lignum sanctum* or "sacred wood." Naturally it was also a source for everyday objects such as bowls, spoons, and wooden clogs. But what it has over other trees is that its bark and branches render fibers from which people from the Stone Age onward made a panoply of strings, ropes, cords, garments, and woven sacks. I recently bought a paintbrush made of a single strip of its wood, not at the hardware store but in a shop of modern chic specializing in garden utensils and fine nature objects.

But don't be fooled by all these feminine attributes. Linden has all the strength to become a majestic tree that towers over many others. One of its characteristics is that the lower branches bow out and grow downward like a giant hooped skirt, which creates a hollow space underneath, enclosed by bright green foliage. This

Pleached linden trees, Belgium.

space was sometimes used as a dance floor at Swiss village festivities not that long ago. In cultivation, the outstanding gift of the docile linden is that it lends itself to being pleached. This means that select branches are trained to grow along a wire in a chosen direction, or sometimes woven into patterns just like espaliered fruit trees: It is a clear advertisement of a gardener's virtuosity. If you have managed yourself a pleached lime walk you've got it made. All your neighbors will tip off their hat to you and ask for your advice.

Death looms large in the somber yew department. This doleful tree is widespread in cemeteries and its timber was used for gallows, Egyptian mummy masks, and coffins. But above all its rot-resistant wood was in great demand for the production of longbows, the main and deadly weapon in Europe throughout the Middle Ages. England and Scotland were the first to run out of supplies; in the process of often and unwisely fighting between themselves they ruthlessly cut down their native stands, sawing off the branch they were sitting on. Thus they were forced to import yew from wherever it could be found, which gave rise to a brisk export business on the continent with trade centers in Danzig and Nuremberg. Between

A group of shaped yew trees at Wethersfield Estate, U.S.A.

Paris parks with their ubiquitous horse chestnut and linden trees

An avenue of maple trees at Storm King Art Center
in New Windsor, New York State

1530 and 1590, Nuremberg alone shipped an estimated 600,000 longbows westwards, made from wood that was acquired or plundered in Germany, Switzerland, and western Russia. By the time firearms replaced the longbow around 1630, Europe had hardly any yew trees left. To make matters worse, yew seeds germinate erratically and the saplings grow at a snail's pace, forever at risk of being chewed down and out by deer and hares. Only after a hundred-year-long lull did they grow back in sufficient quantity to find a more peaceful application in rococo cabinetry and garden furniture.

There is another sinister trait to *Taxus baccata* and that is its serious toxicity. A mere pound of its needles can kill a horse, which is why stable owners systematically eradicate any trace of it in their vicinity. Ironically, the only non-toxic and in fact edible part of this plant is the attractive red "berry," or more precisely the fleshy mantle that encases the poisonous seed: a charming little fruit tailor-made for witches. As so often when the toxic and the medicinal sit side by side, yew was assigned mythical powers, and chips of its wood had talismanic properties. What is interesting in this context is that when modern science replaced mysticism with research, it led to the discovery of taxine as a cure for cancer, thereby balancing out this astonishing plant's dark reputation. In the garden context yew decidedly has clout and people speak of it with awe. It is eminently shapeable and can provide important elements for a garden's framework. But in my view the evergreen needles are too dull; only the young shoots are enchantingly and vividly green, albeit not for very long. But to end on a positive note: Once out of their infancy, yews grow much faster than reputed and their merit as a foil and background for those ravishing English flower borders is hard to beat.

Had my husband and I moved to England or some other botanically benign region instead of to Italy, we surely would have chosen rarer species of trees to surround us. But as things stood, our hands were tied by the availability of plants near the site we had chosen. So we contented ourselves with the common varieties carried by the nurseries not too far away, which also increases their chance of a healthy

An oak walk at Arboretum Kalmthout in Belgium

Magic moment near Central Park South, New York

future. And anyway, once a tree is yours and does well it stops being common. Ad hoc, having gardened for the past twenty-five years in the same spot in Italy, I am gratified by seeing our trees almost fully grown. Contrary to my expectations, it did not take an eternity for them to mature. A given time span looks different depending on the end we look at it from, just as a road offers up a new experience when we drive down it in the opposite direction.

Having moved from one continent to another with a different climate, we had to change gear. Our new property yet again was empty acreage, save for two extraordinary centenarian plane trees on the north side of the house. Whatever trees we were planning to acquire were going to look ridiculously small next to these existing giants. Our first purchases were four lindens and four horse chestnuts; they latched on surprisingly fast, having found a vein of water underground. A white horse chestnut in bloom is a magnificent sight, as is its bold overall design. It originated in Albania

A *Magnolia soulangeana* is waiting for applause. ▶

Room with a view of a red horse chestnut ▶▶
(*Aesculus carnea*) in northern Italy

and, upon proving hardy further north, took Europe by storm and has firmly held its position as the most popular tree in Europe's streets and parks. Sadly it is now prone to leaf miners and diseases we try to conquer, but not always successfully. Since Europe is still traumatized by the Dutch Elm tragedy, we made sure to plant some other members of the chestnut group too, such as two red-flowered horse chestnuts and, at the suggestion of a tree expert, three *Aesculus hippocastanum* "Baumanni." It was not our first choice but a useful compromise as they allegedly are resistant to disease. Their sterile powderpufflike flowers are weird and I do my best to ignore them. Yet their birth-control feature comes in handy, as the conkers of all the others take years to decompose and we are forced to compost them separately. Decidedly unwelcome, on the other hand, are the hordes of young locust trees that have taken over roadsides and woods wherever we are. Since they are massive self-seeders they are now ubiquitous in the whole of Italy, at the expense of many native trees. The *Robinia pseudoacacia* was one of the earliest imports from America in the early 1600s, much admired for its fast growth and strong, durable wood. The annoyance is its wayward offspring, which are a greedy and ruthless lot. Like obstreperous teenagers they talk back to you when you try to control them. Should you cut them down altogether they respond ferociously by resprouting in dragonlike fashion. Their whitish blossoms are banal, but at least their wood is valued for providing the posts in vineyards—another local tradition that is losing ground, giving way to metal or cement. Fruit trees are of course hard to resist, and so we rapidly caved in to apricot and peach trees, persimmons, quinces, and plums. But now, years later, I must confess that they are not nearly as easy to grow as I presumed. Whether on account of drought, or climate change, or the globalization of pests and diseases, I am not overly proud of our orchard. Moreover, once you have visited the splendid Potager du Roi in Versailles, created in 1678 by La

Quintinie for the great Louis, one's own orchard is likely to look embarrassingly shabby by comparison. I rarely include ours when accompanying a visitor on a stroll through the garden. Could I have it over, I would definitely take courses at that famous potager which now is the École nationale supérieure de paysage. Its espaliered fruit trees are sheer works of art.

What I really am keenest on here in my parched valley are trees that guarantee a saturated green in a torrid summer, when many plants begin to look dusty and bedraggled. The three star performers that fulfill that promise are the pomegranate, the fig, and the mulberry.

Statue of Jean de la Quintinie at Potager du Roi

Whether figs and mulberries are cousins or not, they have a lot in common. White sap, for instance, and sweet fruit. Their heart-shaped and deeply-lobed leaves recall Matisse—or the other way round. They are tough and thick, almost like fabric, which must help them to hang on far into the fall. Both figs and mulberries grow into impressive mature trees with dense foliage and do a good job of looking older than they are. In the world of gardens that's a plus! To boot, the fig and the mulberry both have an absolute tolerance to pruning. You can do anything you like with them, chop off this limb or that, turn a tree into a bush, or pare down a shrub to become a tree. True, you may lose the fruit for the next year, but there is a limit to how much mulberry jam you want to make each season. At any rate they bring me great relief from the head-scratching practice of pruning when I am held back by fear that the wrong cut may do everlasting damage. While I am a firm believer in taking instruction from books, reading pruning manuals is an ego-diminishing process, a kind of conspiracy by author and publisher to make us feel like total idiots. Camera manuals translated from the Japanese are in the same category. Theory without demonstration does not work for me. My advice is to turn to a professional in full command of his craft before entrusting the tricky task of pruning to whoever is willing to try. Bad pruning can indeed ruin a tree, or a shrub for that matter.

The third of my lush greens are pomegranate trees, very decorative with their glossy leaves and spangled with fiery red flowers. When I attempt to shorten a few branches that seem to stick out too far, they behave most uncooperatively and send up vertical shoots as straight as arrows instead of forming their normal angular branches, positively interfering with my plan to see them with a rounded head. On account of their beautiful fruits that mature at the end of autumn on bare branches, they are excused. I also know they really would like to be shrubs. In the commercial orchards in China I saw them developed with four main stems just like hazelnuts get handled in Piedmont, our region next door.

Espaliered pear trees, idem

Pinus pinea, the iconic umbrella pine, on the Amalfi coast

Though gray and not green-leafed, I cannot omit the olive from this valuable group of faithful friends in a hot climate. As a prominent player it has defined the landscapes around the Mediterranean basin since classical times, and I can just see Diogenes popping an olive into his mouth as he asks Alexander the Great to step out of the sun. While I had not planned to grow any, I had learnt along the way that olives can safely survive some subzero temperatures. It is humidity and sudden drastic changes in temperature they cannot abide. So I cautiously planted first one small olive tree and then followed with five others, placing them out at the lower end of our hillside to demarcate the border. They had some surprises in store for me, such as a number of varieties to choose from. I stupidly had thought an olive is an olive is an olive. Following the suggestion of a local nursery I had selected "Frantoio." Not being Edith Piaf, regrets inevitably follow me on my heels and no sooner were they planted than I realized I should have chosen "Leccino" instead. They have a greener, flatter leaf and since I am not going to become an oil producer their fruiting aspect is of secondary importance. A real surprise came my way when a heavy snowfall broke some of their thick branches, which were sadly hanging down merely attached by a strip of bark. Having nothing to lose I tied them back up with rope and bandaged them with some duct tape, of all things, and then forgot about the matter. By the middle of the summer the miracle had happened: The broken branches had healed and solidly grown together. "Slow to grow and slow to die" is how olive trees are characterized by Italian farmers. Another time I noticed that the hundreds of olives on my first tree, planted near a south-facing wall, had suddenly shriveled into puckered little balls like dried raisins. I skeptically put a hose trickling down near its roots and for the hell of it left it on all night, while going inside to read up on their pests and diseases. The next morning I found that every single olive had fully plumped up again. The lesson to be learnt is that plants near a building need to be watered twice as often as those out in the open. My watering came in the nick of time. While water surely is the *conditio sine qua non*, in Greek mythology Athena won the contest against Poseidon by applying her godlike magic to have an olive tree spring up from a rock, while her opponent merely produced a source of water. This is why Athenians made her their patroness and named their town after her. The sculpted relief of her triumph was situated on the Parthenon in the tympanum above the entrance, before it was pilfered and brought to northern Europe along with the frieze.

Mysterious H$_2$O

The human body consists of sixty percent water, which is why its importance cannot possibly be overestimated. And we are surrounded by the stuff in even larger quantities, in the form of snow and rain, lakes and rivers, not to mention the sea, which is salty like the liquids within us. As long as we are not overwhelmed by avalanches or floods we regard its presence as a big plus. Any property with access to a shore or a pond carries a higher price tag than just plain acreage with a house on it. Even better than near it is to be IN it, provided it offers a plausible temperature. Floating around in tepid water is a sensuous experience, much enhanced for some of us when we swim naked. The pleasure of skinny dipping might well be a subliminal memory of our prenatal stay in the womb, and I like to think that it was in preparation for such an event that the classic honeymoon destinations were watery locations—particularly Venice in Europe and Niagara Falls in America. Venice is famous for its romantic, placid lagoons, while Niagara's thundering cascades point in the direction of a wild and energetic masculinity. A

Wedding photography in New York's Central Park

The subterranean cistern in El Jadida, Morocco,
was built by the Portuguese in 1514.

century and a half ago these settings were meant to help newlyweds through the
difficult first steps of cohabitation, far away from the prying eyes of relatives at
home. And as a boon the aforementioned locations offered picturesque backdrops
for the young couples to be eternalized by that fashionable new craft, photography.

Some of my earliest memories are the distant days of our summer vacations spent
in the mountains of the canton of Valais in southwestern Switzerland, where traditions,
including farming, had remained unchanged for generations. The locals had devised an
irrigation system to deal with the typical summer droughts in the form of a network of
small canals, about a foot wide, called *bisses*, through which glacial water rushed with
amazing force and speed. This unforgettable playground was filled with suspense for
my brothers and me, as toys placed on the lively water at a selected spot would race
away in the horizontal canal to be intercepted at another designated point further away.
The thrill was provided by the looming danger of an item getting lost if that second

station was manned by someone clumsy. To reduce the possibility of such mini disasters we sent a dry leaf or twig ahead as a warning of more important shipments to come: little boats, rubber ducks, rafts with matchbox cars on them, or an occasional piece of dollhouse furniture on a wobbly base. These dramatic ventures left us drenched, drained, and thoroughly exhilarated, except when a cherished object disappeared in the water's vortex never to be retrieved again. The graphic TV footage of the record-shattering tsunami in 2011 uncannily recalled those long-gone images of our miniature toys tossed around and swallowed by the *bisses* above Grimentz in Val d'Anniviers.

Another event I remember with clarity was the magnificent magic show at the Corso Theater in Zurich. Spiffily dressed conjurers performed all those tricks with colored handkerchiefs, rabbits and hats, knots undone and women sawn in half, which kept everyone spellbound and openmouthed. But the simplest of all demonstrations was the one I liked best. One of the artists managed to make a thin stream of colored water jump out of a jug in a wide arc into another one and then back again without losing a drop. Skill and not deception was the name of that game. You could will water to behave the way you wanted. When transferring liquids in the kitchen from a large spout into a small opening without a funnel I occasionally apply the positive mental force of the "yes we can" that I first saw in that circuslike performance. If you concentrate on paying attention and have a steady hand it works. Doing it in an arc, however, takes something more.

A happy camper

More magic was added fifty years later when a slew of particularly scorching Italian summers impressed the need for water on us yet again. The public *acquedotto*—evoking visions of ancient Roman stone aqueducts—was simply a black rubber hose running alongside the unpaved country road, and as it did not deliver sufficient quantities to us we decided to look around for a diviner. After a lengthy search by word of mouth we found such a talent, known as a *rabdomante* in Italian. He showed up with his brother, who did not have the same ability but gave moral support and at the end of the procedure collected the money the diviner himself was not allowed to touch. Disappointingly, the essential tool was not a hazel rod but just a piece of wire. At least I was allowed to put my hand on that of the *rabdomante* once the wire started to twitch. It did so with palpable force. After half an hour's intense divining a promising spot made itself known halfway down the sloping field, and then the real performance began. The diviner kept his eyes closed, looking inward I suppose. His brother explained that every strike of the gadget indicated a depth of ten meters. Mystic measurements tied to the metric system seemed weird. At every stroke of the wire the man did a little stomping dance, a bit like the villain getting shot dead in cowboy movies with his feet bouncing around for a few more frames before he crashes to the ground. After seven dances and tension-loaded intervals the spectacle was finished, leaving the *rabdo* exhausted. We paid his brother the suggested small sum that amounted to a third of a ticket to La Scala. That was fair enough, as we only got the first act. The second act was that we had to pay the full fee in advance to the construction firm that was going to drill at the discovered spot, regardless of whether they hit water or not. The third act was that once the pump was working it produced a pathetic squirt of water every twenty seconds. Comedy or tragedy? Who is to say. A few years later Larry applied plain logic and we had a proper well and a pump installed at the bottom of our property. It still does yeoman's duty for most of the year.

Water tamed and harnessed in massive quantities for utilitarian purposes is handled differently from the small proportion that finds its way into our gardens. Here it becomes a highlight and is carefully positioned where its supernatural extra, namely the ability to mirror, is made the most of. A smooth surface reflects the sky and clouds above and plants and buildings nearby. Besides increasing light and expanding space, it provides motion, which is tantamount to saying: entertainment. Thanks to its movements, water works as a vehicle of sound. If sound is what we are after, we have to forgo that placid surface and address the engineering challenges of how to make the water rise or fall as soaring jets or gushing cascades, or construct a series of narrow canals descending at various angles, thereby hitting different notes

◄ The water tank at Palácio Fronteira in Lisbon is magnificently adorned with blue azulejo tiles, depicting victorious horsemen.

Then...

whenever their contents drip onto a new level, just like a musical instrument. Splashing fountains and spluttering noises are ever present in piazzas and patios in the South, where with Pavlovian predictability they refresh us with their melodious rhythms even before we dip our hands into the cool liquid.

Odd as this observation may seem, water can only be carried around without a vessel when it becomes ice, and a body of water is actually defined by what surrounds it. Landscape architects and builders design basins, fountains, canals, rills, or whatever the client fancies. Being manmade, these chosen containers are influenced by the trends and fashions

that are or were in the air at the time of their creation and neatly parallel the history of art and architecture. Usually made from stone, they are the elements that contribute to a garden's skeleton and rival the longevity of trees. Able to survive centuries of neglect, they become meaningful vestiges of the past, in places where hardly anything else evidences the pleasure ground that had existed in that spot. How interesting that the infuriatingly elusive substance H_2O gave rise to some of the more permanent remnants of garden history.

The idea of diverting water into large cisterns and storage pools was undoubtedly key in bringing civilization about. Ornamentation cannot have lagged far behind when the construction of such reservoirs was undertaken, as a means of celebrating the existential necessity of their content. Ancient Persia and Egypt—both countries with a hot climate and vast expanses of deserts and arid land—give us quite a bit of information about the earliest gardens we know of. It is no surprise that the idea of a green oasis made by man was first born and formulated there. The Persian word for "paradise" is the same as that for "garden" and stands for a peaceful enclosure bordered by high walls, replete with refreshing air and cooling shade, and full of delightful trees, flowering carpets, the ever-present sound of tinkling water, and singing birds. All these luxuries depend on the presence of water: constant irrigation is the *conditio sine qua non*. It is worth mentioning here that the geometry of a rectangle divided into four quarters formed by the two straight "rivers" of the Persian garden is a symbolic pattern, but it is also tied to the practicality of straight canals, connecting water tanks and fountains in order to distribute the precious fluid evenly over the whole surface. Trees planted alongside the canals emphasize that regular grid, which is often the motif in the evocative Persian carpets. The traditional plan of a cultivated rectangle fanned out from Persia in all directions, and was taken up and elaborated by the Muslim Arabs when they conquered large parts of the old world. Thanks to the Moorish forays into Europe we have a splendid example of their garden style, which today is visited by thousands of people when touring Spain. You can't miss the message at the Alhambra, that famous Islamic legacy in Andalusia. No matter how impressive its Byzantine architecture, water is its main theme. It unites its courtyards and outdoor spaces, every one of which is adorned by a differently shaped fountain or basin. Narrow channels known as rills sometimes link two sections, and occasionally we encounter one of these grooves coursing through a building to join the sunlight again when coming out on the other side. Though the plantings of the Alhambra and the Generalife are not what they used to be 700 years ago, the ubiquitous sight and sound of water have not lost their allure and enchant everyone without fail.

Taking a quantum leap forward to the Italian Renaissance, a period that became a triumphant expression of man's affirmation as the center of the universe and allowed pleasures to be gotten from all aspects of life, we see that garden making proliferated in Italy. The Church and the aristocracy, with the Medici family at their helm, had all that was needed to make that sector flourish: wealth, a benign climate, an abundance of water, fertile soil, and access to the best architects and sculptors of their day. And they did not have to reach back as far as Persia for inspiration. They had ruins and remnants at their doorstep, the Emperor Hadrian's palatial villa and gardens in Tivoli for instance, and they had literature, spearheaded by Pliny's accounts of his own gardens and bodies of water in Lazio and Tuscany. By the middle of the sixteenth century, running water in the garden had become a regular feature. A landscape architect would keep a *fontaniere* as his right-hand man, a hydraulic engineer who in all likelihood had acquired his basic knowledge through studying the first-century treatise on how to build aqueducts and underground systems of pipes to transport water to its destination, which could be quite far away. Water was instrumental in making the newest inventions work, including automata and all sorts of gadgets that were designed to enliven many sites. This ability to entertain was taken to unimaginable heights at Villa d'Este in Tivoli, a stone's

The enchanting nympheum and garden pavilions of ►
Villa Litta Lainate have been saved in the nick of time,
and the refreshing *giochi d'aqua* are working again.

throw away from Hadrian's villa. After Cardinal Ippolito II d'Este had acquired the valley and steep hillside for his retirement, he spent the next twelve years developing the garden in the High Renaissance style. He engaged Pirro Ligorio, an architect with a thorough knowledge of Roman antiquities, to help him create an extravagant showplace and fill it to the brim with the most spectacular waterworks ever seen. Fanciful attractions awaited the visitor on every terrace, and a complicated network formed by axes, cross-axes, and paths added to the fun of finding the Fountain of the Dragons, the Oval Fountain, the Owl Fountain, the Organ Fountain, the esplanade of fishponds presenting a curtain of water to hide behind, the Avenue of a Hundred Fountains, which is the most famous of them all, and finally the Rometta Fountain, a miniature replica of Rome and its monuments, not forgetting the Diana of Ephesus with her numerous water-squirting breasts. Many of the artworks were equipped with hydraulic devices to fill the air with birdsong and wondrous sounds of all kinds, and, needless to say, these gadgets depended on waterpower to make them work. A veritable Disneyland both then and now, this amazing place is still worth visiting. A popular adjunct of this and other gardens were the so-called *giochi d'acqua*, where hidden spouts would suddenly spring into action and spray water from behind, below, or above at the unsuspecting guests, eliciting squeals and laughter, and possibly present them with an excuse to get out of some of their soaked garments. This baroque idea of fun spread throughout Europe and remained a popular garden feature until around 1900.

Another rare jewel of Renaissance art is Cardinal Gambara's garden at Villa Lante, believed to have been designed by the famous architect Vignola, maybe with some input by the cardinal himself. After all, they both were Renaissance men, which is to say highly cultivated people with many talents. Cardinal Gambara had commissioned Vignola to take the construction of his summer residence in hand, in the cooling hills near Viterbo, not far from Palazzo Farnese in Caprarola. Vignola's decision to make use of water as the main central axis of his plan was ingenuous. Springing forth from the woods above the villa in the guise of a primordial source, it falls first into a pond before continuing downhill, occasionally disappearing then resurging again, sometimes smoothly, at other times gurgling, taking various forms at it weaves in and out of our view. Its course takes it from the deep shade of the upper terraces to an intermediate area of dappled light, from where it softly descends to its final destination in radiant sunshine. It ends on a large terrace formed by a square water basin set in an embroidered parterre, in the middle of which we perceive a central round island that forms the base of the final highlight, which was completed by Gambara's successor Cardinal Montalto, who managed to sneak in his own coat of arms: the sculpture of four glorious wet young men, rising up from yet another fountain and jubilantly holding up their emblem to the blue sky. This is the scene people behold first when they enter the garden today from the street outside.

The water's function as the vertebra of the site is not immediately obvious, and best studied when beginning the tour from the upper end of the garden, where it is initially admired in a fountain adorned with dolphins, masks, and vases. It then goes underground and unexpectedly issues forth a few steps later from under the pavement, splashing down in the center of a stepped ramp and contained by parallel scrolls somewhat resembling crayfish, in a reference to Gambara's name. After hiding out again we next encounter it carrying the axis through the large fountain of the river gods, to then continue through the center of the long stone table with its built-in rectangular trough for cooling wine. The observant visitor will calculate that this perfect al fresco dining situation, undoubtedly a spot of great merriment in partial shade, is located exactly in the middle of the main axis. Another basin picks up the water theme once more at the next level down. More fountains and water niches can be seen throughout the garden, achieving that much praised equilibrium of water, nature, and architecture that makes Villa Lante the paragon of Renaissance gardens. As a well-preserved masterpiece of rare harmony and refinement it remains one of the great treasures of Italy.

Some years later, the delicious refinement and relative intimacy of Italian landscape architecture were transformed in France, when a change of scale took hold of European rulers' minds. Vying with each other to build ever more impressive parks and waterworks, they were fueled by an unquenchable desire for ostentation. Louis XIV handled that PR race easily and won. Notwithstanding that his terrain at Versailles was flat and soggy and had to be drained to make it workable, he managed to turn endless muddy ground into parkland by employing armies of engineers, sculptors, and artisans. Water not being a rarity per se in northern France, plenty of ornate masonry and statuary was introduced for special effect: showmanship. Practical considerations were not at the forefront of the king's thinking, and by the time the plans were completed the water pressure was insufficient to keep all his fountains running at the same time. As an aside I would like to add that competitive zeal in horticulture is by no means limited to aristocracy. There are some hobby gardeners, too, who are beavering away at growing the biggest pumpkins and straightest carrots, or seeking to come up with a rare new hybrid flower. The impulse to win is deeply ingrained in human endeavors.

It is inherent not just in *Homo sapiens* but in nature and evolution itself. Biggest, however, is not necessarily best; the size and scale has to fit the subject. Château de Vaux-le-Vicomte is a case in point, as it has a much smaller park than Versailles yet one that is more distinguished and served as its inspiration. But as things typically pan out in life, all the other kings, dukes, and emperors in Europe wanted to have their own little Versailles, not their Vaux-le-Vicomte or Courances, nor any of the other ravishing French chateaux of that time. Status is not tied to good taste, but to power.

A new wind blew in when the Age of Enlightenment worked its force not only on science and philosophy but also on esthetics, which included advice on how to view nature. It caused a truly revolutionary development in the world of English gardens. When the horizons of science were expanded, the idea was applied to the landscape quite literally, too. Walls and fences came down with a vengeance to reveal simplified scenes further away. The much-touted ha-has (which had previ-

The Grove of Apollo's Baths is one of the highlights at Versailles.

ously been called trenches, or s*aut de loup* in French) helped rein in distant views so that they would seem to have become part of the garden, which as a result looked as if it had melted into the countryside. Agriculture was sentimentalized and grazing cows and sheep were lured to come quite close to front yards. This new approach to gardening was heavily underpinned by philosophy and poetry. It was enthusiastically proclaimed by people who were educated and articulate, property owners and architects among them. The garden was intellectualized. Much ink flowed extolling the radical new style, but some dissenting voices were heard, too. It also got a new name: landskip. The poet Alexander Pope wielded considerable influence on the new movement and his garden in Twickenham on the River Thames was something of a showpiece. In what were really large parks rather than gardens, the desired scenes were pastoral meadows, open groves and green glades, clumps of trees, originally inspired by the classical paintings of Nicolas Poussin and Claude Lorrain, whose landscapes incidentally were Italian rather than French or English, and had been painted a hundred years earlier (all roads lead to Rome).

The many imitations of Versailles reached a peak at Palazzo Reale di Caserta.

The deceptively simple
trickle at the top of Villa
Lante is headed for a
glorious performance of
many acts further down.

The River Cherwell in
Oxfordshire became a major
player in the English
landscape revolution
of the eighteenth century.

William Kent added a
conceptual note to his
design at Rousham in
the form of this narrow
curved rill.

Maybe the new style was born in England on account of its green surface, which lent itself marvelously to the new fashion, and because its climate had more water than Italy, which facilitated the creation of lakes and faster growth of trees. Water, with its many moods, was a prominent player and came in every shape and form. Lakes, particularly irregularly shaped ones, rivers, streams, brooks, natural springs, and ponds were essential additions to these idealized settings, with their gentle hills and valleys as well as sinuous lines that led to specific views. Meandering paths gave visitors the chance to take slow strolls near lakes and rivers on long summer afternoons, stopping off at selected spots to inhale what nature offered and to experience the emotions—or at least hope to do so—suggested by whatever the clever landskip architect had dreamed up. William Kent, for one, made himself a lasting name when he "leaped the fence and saw that all nature was a garden," loudly abhorring the straight line per se. The River Cherwell at Rousham in Oxfordshire was much to his liking, with its two sweeping bends. He took full advantage of it, happy to follow in the footsteps of Charles Bridgeman, who had made the original plans for the owners, which Kent then elaborated and augmented. Bare nature by itself did not quite suffice to set people's imagination in motion, so statuary, eye-catchers, and temples, many with links to mythology, were added in order to enhance the sense of mysticism. Romanticism is about yearning for another place and time. Sculptures and occasionally odd constructions were strategically positioned along the circuit the visitor was supposed to follow. At Rousham, Venus's Vale was a place for the visitor to stop and gaze on a sunlit descent, before continuing to the Cold Bath complete with bathhouse, and the narrowest of curving rills at the dark heart of a shady woodland patch. These romantic sentiments were also amply catered for at two other famous landskip parks, Stowe in Buckinghamshire and Stourhead in Wiltshire. They boast larger temples, bridges, cascades, and arcades than Rousham, and have big lakes, too. Of course, they also harked back to Roman times, sometimes combined with a touch of English moralism as insinuated by the Temple of British Worthies at Stowe.

A good case can be made to compare those Elysian landscapes to stage sets, within which, like in the theater, human emotions are provoked and coaxed towards specific climaxes, be they drama or laughter or reconciliation. The ecstasy felt when a rare outdoor view in spectacular light opens up to you is a similar occurrence, comparable to the final embrace at the end of the play. Since water was on the up and up in all forms, bridges that had not previously been needed in

Lyegrove, Badminton, England ►
Neoclassical French
Contemporary Switzerland

Lush display of moisture-loving plants on a pond
in the Hamptons on Long Island near New York

gardens became a swell introduction, ranging from more humble models through
an entire plethora of possibilities to the elegant import from Italy. To take one
example of the latter, the Palladian style was chosen for the majestic bridge in
Stourhead which has since become well known as one of the film locations for
Barry Lyndon and the 2005 production of *Pride and Prejudice.*

Another big wheel among the garden architects of that period was the capable
Lancelot Brown, who went to work for Lord Cobham at Stowe in 1741 to expand
upon what his predecessors Bridgeman and Kent had hitherto achieved. It is a
historically important park that has gone through several phases of change but
remains fairly intact on the whole, and can still be viewed as the ideal landskip
that inspired its creation. "Capability" Brown subsequently set himself up as an
independent landscaper. While he was an excellent designer, he must have also
been a persuasive businessman, for he designed and redesigned 200 estates during

◄ Bog plants such as *Rodgersia aesculifolia,*
Astilboides tabularis, Alchemica mollis
at the edge of a pond in Normandy

Kilouna Farm's elliptical pond, surrounded by massive
amounts of azaleas, was one of Russell Page's masterpieces.

A swimming pool in the Hudson Valley, New York

Stepping close up we discover David Hockney's brush strokes.

his lifetime. Today there is a great deal of affected indignation about all the previous gardens he tossed out in the process. But maybe not all of those 200 discarded lots were that wonderful; perhaps they were on their last leg and going to seed. Yet I can understand the dismay as I have seen twentieth-century gardeners nearly weep when forced by a director to rip out a carefully tended hedge, or to alter an immaculate lawn to create a hollow in the middle that would make the greensward more interesting. Change sometimes seems like sheer folly and caprice. It is a drawback in our life that we cannot have and keep everything—and even worse that we cannot take it with us when we go. However, to embrace a new movement rather than continuously bemoan what is no longer there may keep us a little younger while we are still around.

An appendage to the eighteenth-century water mania is or was the grotto and its little sister, the nymphaeum. Grottoes have existed since Roman times and could be found in many places, especially in France and Italy. Their true origins were caves and groves in ancient Greece, magical sacrosanct places in beautiful spots with views that needed no further help. Venerable trees may have supplied shade and divine associations. Over time, grottoes in other cultures became highly decorated and were equipped with cascading water or a fountain inside that would add intriguing sounds to the eerie atmosphere. Its walls were rusticated and richly encrusted with shells and colorful pebbles or stones that glittered when hit by light. Sometimes they were near the sea and got flooded at high tide. Alexander Pope had an important one in his garden near the Thames, and thus it became fashionable for the wealthy to have one too. The grotto must have been something of a status symbol, and supposedly was a place to retreat to. The nymphaeum was different: consecrated to nymphs, beautiful young women who dwelled near streams, rivers, lakes, and the sea, they were usually associated with springs. Nymphaeums tended to be semi-open rooms with vaulted ceilings and an apse that resembled the shape of grottoes. They were used as gathering places rather than retreats. The closest I ever got to possessing such a building was at our Old Apple Farm in Katonah, which had something called the Spring House. I thought its name referred to my favorite season and in my foolish fantasy saw slender young women in transparent garments, flower wreaths wound around their heads, performing art nouveau dances in April or May. But on closer inspection the "spring house" was merely a rundown one-room shack that was sinking into the wetland in a patch of watercress. The latter was served when we were having tea at our first visit as potential buyers, in the form of triangular little watercress sandwiches that were casually described as coming "from our garden." A few visits later we bought the place, watercress and all. But I suspect the spring house must have rotted away on its swampy ground since then, and, alas, no Rites of Spring were ever celebrated there.

The eighteenth-century Landscape Movement exerted massive influence on our time as the majority of public parks have enthusiastically taken over its esthetic. The former grand gardens of the wealthy English have their equivalent today in public parks practically everywhere. F. L. Olmstead certainly was influenced by his landscape tour to England in 1850 before he began to design that most wonderful of all parks, Central Park in Manhattan, New York, with many other parks and urban projects in America to follow. In France, private and public places followed suit to create the *jardin à l'anglaise.* The Italians accepted the *prato inglese* into their vocabulary, a term that actually refers to a proper lawn, though theirs are never as perfect as those exposed to English drizzle. The Germans go for the *englischer Garten*, and so on and on. The eighteenth-century romance with antiquity was left behind; now the trees, meadows, and undulating terrain became highlights. The passion for water also survives, in somewhat altered form. The natural landskip ponds, for instance, had bare banks, whereas the gardeners I know today are eager to furnish the edge of their pond with moisture-loving plants. Mythology has less of a pull while smaller plants have gained in importance, and modern sculptures are added.

Another subject, the bathhouse, was well documented in Roman times as a place that would be visited daily. Harems in the Ottoman Empire similarly had baths and pools to keep the odalisques fully occupied for a large part of the day. Curiously, the bathhouse entered people's consciousness in England only in the eighteenth century through the Landscape Movement. But now that we are surrounded by an abundance of public and private swimming pools in our lives, they have become ubiquitous. The swimming pools are, as I stated above about bodies of water in general, defined by what surrounds them. They come in many variants, and it is well worth calling in a garden designer for suggestions. As for water in our own garden, the swimming pool is suitably integrated and barely visible from elsewhere. We do not have a fountain, nor a gazebo, nor sculptures nor any other complication. We live between our farmhouse buildings, which set the tone, with chopped wood, bales of hay, and trees and shrubs. As for a water feature, my only item is the garden hose, an indispensable friend. And so to this very day, the 22nd of February 2024, the sweetest music of all is still not the sound of rushing rivers and cascades but the raindrops drumming on the roof after an extended drought, followed by the ecstasy with which this tale began, and which has now come full circle.

The End

Notes

A general remark: Italy, France, and England have myriad gardens and very good garden guide books, which I am sure other countries have too. Needless to say, Googling is also a valid option, and it may be a good idea to check opening times and other details on the Internet before setting out on an excursion.

pp.6–10 The black and white photographs in this chapter were all taken before I was born. The letter addressed to me at Parco Grifeo 38, where I spent some holidays when I was very young, before the villa was sold and torn down, was the only one I could find with that address, which made this vanished place more real for me.

pp.24–25 Aerial photograph taken over Île-de-France, the region that surrounds Paris.

p.26 Brooklyn Botanical Garden in New York City was designed by the Olmstead brothers and is very large. It has many sections and three Japanese gardens, of which one is famous for its cherry blossoms. It is also a great learning institution with many publications.

p.27 Old Westbury Gardens, Long Island, New York, is the former private garden of the Phipps family and was converted into a museum in 1959. It is open for tours between April and October, and is a perfect setting for weddings too.
Tel: +1 516 333 0048

pp.28–29 The color of the Bougainvillea stems not from the flower, but from its bracts, which are colorfast, as flowers in the tropics have to be too. Saturated pastel shades hail from cooler climates; a surplus of sun would bleach them.

p.32 In subtropical climates, tulip and daffodil bulbs have to spend a couple of months in the refrigerator before they get planted.

p.33 Not a Japanese cherry tree, but the fruiting variety called "Duroni di Vignola" that makes big, black cherries.

p.34 Lamb House in Rye, England, was Henry James's country home in his old age. It is a National Trust property and can be visited.

p.37 Schloss Bothmar near Malans in Switzerland is at an altitude of c. 600 m above sea level. Mountain climates can be rude and limit your choice of plants. Schloss Bothmar happens to be in a protected spot, and its late resident, the poet Flandrina von Salis used to refer to it as "my Riviera." Visits by appointment: Tel: +41 81 32 22 102

p.38 These Lilies of the Nile (*Agapanthus*) were planted by Contessa Giuppi Pietriomarchi beneath her olive trees at La Ferriera in Capalbio, Italy. An inspired combination. Blue irises among olive trees are more common. See notes for p.100

p.40 The island of Martha's Vineyard in Massachusetts has extremely high humidity in summer time.

p.44 Carl von Linne's garden in Uppsala, Sweden, open to the public, is the northernmost garden I visited and photographed.

p.46 The *vivaio* of Anna Peyron and her daughter Saskia in Castagneto near Turin is a recommendable nursery specialized in roses, dahlias, selected rare flowers, and shrubs.
Tel: +39 338 787 0820

p.67 The Portuguese Quinta de Bacalhôa Palace and Museum, not far from Lisbon, was once a royal abode. Its decorative water tank is surrounded by a splendid garden. Now in private hands it can be visited, especially as it is also a winery and does weddings. For appointments: bacalhoa.pt

p.69 Hall Barn in Buckinghamshire, England, is a historic country seat with a formal garden that dates to the seventeenth century. It comprises large woods, ancient yew hedges, and an ornamented obelisk, of which a detail is shown.

p.71 I visit allotment gardens whenever and wherever I can find them as their lighthearted atmosphere is very amusing. None of the sweat other gardeners experience.

pp.72–73 No caption needed. Just look at how much work goes into well-tempered gardens.

p.74 The Emmenthal region in Switzerland is an area full of rural traditions well worth visiting.

p.77 Villa Gamberaia in Settignano has a meticulously kept sixteenth/seventeenth-century garden, with ancient holm oaks, an attractive *limonaia*, and very nice stonework, as seen on p.103. It overlooks Florence and can be visited from May to October, reservation required. Be advised that there is no parking nearby.
Tel: +39 055 697205
villagamberaia.com

p.80 This comment may be a bit far fetched, but French working garments were traditionally called *les bleus*, which is what the gardeners in the image on the right wear. The fabric originally was called "bleu de Nimes" to denote where it came from, and now it is known as denim.

The blue shades of the Thailandese woman on the left probably have a different origin. In the Far East, blue was derived from plants, frequently of the *Indigofera* genus, but this one here might be different.

p.83 The traditional folk festival in Bern, Switzerland, named the "Ziibelemärit" takes place every year on the fourth Monday in November.

p.84 Giardino Giusti in Verona, on the left bank of the River Adige, has been the property of the Giusti family since 1400. As one of the finest late Renaissance gardens it is famous for its Viale di Cipressi leading to the palace up high. It can be visited and is very close to the center of Verona. Tel: +39 45 803 4029

p.84 The Met Cloisters, as it is called, is a museum in Upper Manhattan in Fort Tryon Park, New York City. It specializes in European medieval art and architecture and has three authentic cloisters. Among the many Romanesque and Gothic objects it also owns the Unicorn Tapestries, which are on a par with the French equivalents at Musée de Cluny in Paris.

pp.90–91 At the very top of the list of Italian treasures is the government-owned Palazzo Farnese in Caprarola near Viterbo, designed by the architect Giacomo Barozzi da Vignola, who also was active at the nearby Villa Lante. Its showpieces are the fortresslike palazzo with its formal surroundings, and the tucked away parterre garden near the Casino (sometimes called Villa Farnese or Palazzina), which was Cardinal Alessandro Farnese's private pleasure pavilion. Trees, clipped hedges, *canephori*, i.e. caryatids with baskets on their head, sunny walks, and low stone walls with benches to sit on are

a rare delight. Its silence makes you feel transported back to the heart of the Italian Rinascimento.

p.94 The French Château de Villandry is 15 km west of Tours, on the banks of the Loire, and is open to the public daily. You should go there more than once since the vegetables undergo seasonal changes. Tel: +33 247 500 209

p.96 The National Trust property Sissinghurst Castle in Cranbrook, Kent, England, is of course a must. Tel: +44 1580 710701

p.99 Dumbarton Oaks Research Library and Collection and its garden is in the Georgetown neighborhood of Washington D.C. and open to the public. Tel: +1 202 339 6400

p.100 La Ferriera is Contessa Giuppi Pietromarchi's country seat in Capalbio in the Maremma (Tuscany and Lazio), where she has gardened for over fifty years. Botanical interest runs in her blood as her maiden name was Sgaravatti (merchants of seeds and bulbs, the Italian equivalent of Vilmorin in France). Her knowledge of horticulture was further increased as the wife of the diplomat Count Antonio Pietromarchi, who was ambassador to Morocco and Holland, and through visiting many other countries as well. giuppi.pietromarchi@gmail.com

p.102 The painter Jennifer Bartlett died in 2022 and I do not know what became of her roof garden. She certainly was a powerhouse who could also express herself with plants. One of her projects was planning a public garden in Battery Park, which unfortunately was not executed.

p.103 La Mortella on the island of Ischia, an exotic paradise created by

Russell Page for the composer William Walton and his wife Susanna. Since 1991 it has been open to the public. lamortella.org See notes for p.77 and p.99.

p.107 and p.123 A grass garden in Watermill, Long Island, New York, was created by Wolfgang Oehme and James van Sweden for Mr. and Mrs. Alex and Carol Rosenberg in the early 1980s. At the helm for this new type of planting it became a brilliant showpiece in the States, and may well still be.

p.109 The wheat grain called farro has its equivalent named spelt (*Triticum spelta, Triticum dicoccum,* and *Triticym monococcum*).

p.110 When Le Notre took the making of Versailles in hand, between five and six thousand horses were employed just for the rough work.

pp.112–113 *Left*: women emptying out a rice paddy by hand, bucket by bucket, is a common sight in Vietnam. *Center:* Fields of rice seedlings which at the right moment get pulled up and turned into small bundles. *Right*: The small bundles are brought to the flooded paddies, where the workers stick each seedling separately into the soft muddy earth.

p.118 Skansen, the open-air museum in Stockholm, Sweden, has existed since 1891 and has an abundance of rural houses with interiors to show Swedish life before the Industrial Revolution.

p.122 Mount Vernon, George and Martha Washington's stately home, is 25 km from Washington D.C. in Virginia. Tel:+1 780-2000.

p.123 See note for p.107

p.125 *Left:* Alrecht Duerer, "Das grosse Rasenstück" at the Albertina museum in Vienna. *Right:* Hieronymus Bosch, *The Haycart* (slightly cropped), the middle panel of the triptych at the Prado Museum in Madrid.

pp.132–136 For information about the Infiorata contact the Pro Loco Spello office in Umbria, Italy.
Tel: +39 742 301 009

p.142 Longwood Gardens in Brandywine Creek Valley in Pennsylvania is a huge botanical garden and it will take four hours to explore all of it. It has many events and many visitors.
longwoodgardens.org
Tel: +1 610 388 1000

p.148 Charleston Manor, Sussex, England. Tel: +44 132 381 1626; Claude Monet's house and garden in Giverny are widely known and have become something of a shrine for art and-garden pilgrims. Find out about prices and how to get there on the Internet, or email contact@claudemonetgiverny.fr
Tel: +33 2 32 51 28 21;

p.149 Arley Hall is a stately home in Cheshire, England. It is a venerable old place with a 600-year-old tithe barn and many different gardens. The magnificent double herbaceous border is said to be the oldest in England, and therefore must be the oldest one in the world.
arleyhallandgardens.com;
The Gardens of Ninfa, 64 km from Rome, are an Italian natural monument, where the art of gardening is combined with old ruins. It is a most unusual, very large and romantic place. Book tickets ahead of time.
Tel: +39 773 188 0888

p.156 I have a faint recollection that I photographed this *Lupinus arboreus* at one of England's truly wonderful gardens, Great Dixter. The house was built by Edwin Lutyens and opened in 1912. Its late owner, Christopher Lloyd, was a very experienced gardener and a well-known garden writer.
Tel: +44 1797 253 107

p.158 Photographed at New York Botanical Garden in the Bronx, which was established in 1891 and comprises 250 acres, and the Enid A. Haupt Conservatory, which offers splendid exhibitions such as their orchid shows between February and April.
Tel: +1 718 817 8700

p.160 Villa Melzi d'Eril, Bellagio, on Lake Como.

p.161 *Right:* the rhododendron, magnolia, and camellia garden of the late Sir Peter Smithers. For visits to the garden contact the Municipio di Vico Morcote, Switzerland.

pp.162–163 Photographed near Castello Balduino di Monalto di Pavia in Italy.

p.165 Green Animals Topiary Garden is in Portsmouth, Rhode Island.
Tel: +1 401 683 1267

p.172 Sir Peter Smithers, the English diplomat, having lived and gardened in different climates, was the most accomplished gardener I knew. He believed that one should make the necessary efforts to inform oneself and aspire to grow the best type of plants that could be found. All this he explained in great detail in his book *The Adventure of a Gardener.*

p.175 The white wisteria grows in Old Westbury Gardens on Long Island, New York. See note for p.27.

p.179 The Alhambra hardly needs any explanation, but try not to visit it on big holidays.

pp.184–185 Our house was built near Millbrook in the Hudson Valley. The picture shows its east side and how well it is ensconced in a slight hollow in the landscape of soft hills.

p.201 The high hedge of Albertine roses forming a circle was the beginning of a large rose garden planted by my friends Maddalena Piccinini and Filippo Gugliemo in the hills near Piacenza.

pp.204–205 The very gifted and multitalented designer Federico Forquet keeps adding new splendors to the house and garden he created with his late partner Matteo Spinola at Valle Pinciole near Cetona, in Tuscany. It is a breathtaking place and will most likely be taken over by the FAI, the Italian equivalent of the English National Trust.

p.210 *Left:* The botanical name of the Indian bean tree is *Catalpa bignonioides*, a native of North America and China. *Right:* The honeysuckle is *Lonicera japonica* "Halliana," extremely floriferous and fragrant, as is the nameless English rose intertwined with it.

p.212 An apple at Le Potager du Roi, see note pp. 237-38

p.214 An oasis like this one is my idea of Eden.

p.215 Central Park in New York City was created by F.L. Olmstead, who began the work in 1858. Full of botanical riches, it is worth touring it with a tree guidebook in hand.

p.216 I suggest reading about the complicated metabolism of the tropical *Ficus benghalensis* and *Ficus macrophylla* in a botanical book.

p.217 What you see at Angkor Wat are undoubtedly the most photographed aerial roots of *Ficus* trees in the world.

p.219 Marco Vaccaroni, our tree surgeon, is from Piacenza and climbs trees without a ladder.

p.220 *Cornus florida* "Cherokee Chief" has very large petals and is particularly disease resistant.

p.221 The crabapple tree growing near the garden designer Nancy McCabe's house in Connecticut is richly colored. *Malus* or "Flowering Crabs" comprise a genus of some twenty-five species of deciduous, small-to-medium-sized trees that enchant us with their blossoms, fruit, and an abundance of seasonal charms.

p.223 The formal walk between sugar maples and sculptures backed by a massive hedge is one of the Wethersfield Estate & Gardens' main features. The late Chauncey Devereux Stillman's large property on 257 Pugsley Hill Road, Amenia, in Dutchess County, New York, can now be visited.
Tel: +1 845 373 8037

p.227 This group of yew trees at Wethersfield Estate and Gardens are hardier than the traditional *Taxus baccata*. They are *Taxus x media* "Hatfieldii" or "Hicksii."

p.228 Seen here are trees at the Jardin des Tuileries and Jardin du Luxembourg in Paris. Other than linden and horse chestnuts, plane trees are also often seen in French parks.

p.230 Storm King Art Center is an open-air museum and sculpture park in New Windsor, New York State. Reserve tickets in advance.
Tel: +1 845 534 3115

p.231 The trees flanking the walk are *Quercus robur*. Their size makes

you guess that Arboretum Kalmthout in Belgium is one of the oldest tree and plant gardens in Flanders.
Tel: +32 3 666 67 41
info@arboretumkalmthout.be

p.237 Le Potager du Roi, 4, rue Hardy, 78000 Versailles was created in 1678 by Jean de la Quintinie for the sun king and is still cultivated and well kept. It became the Ecole nationale superieure d'horticulture in 1874 and then in 1976 the Ecole nationale superieure du paysage. Not only can it be visited, but sometimes, on particular days, they their surplus fruits and vegetables days, their sale.
Tel. +33 1 39 02 71 03 (or 39 51 61 29).

p.244 The impressive garden of the Palácio Fronteira with its famous water reservoir has one of the world's most beautiful blue tile (azulejo) collections and must not be missed. It is in Lisbon itself, and anybody can tell you where it is. Tel: ¹351 21 778 2023

p.246 The naked lady, probably Venus, is taking her bath in the romantic woodland setting of Palazzo Reale di Caserta, the royal palace and park constructed by Luigi Vanvitelli (1700-1773) for the Bourbon King of Naples. It is huge, located 35 km north of Naples.

p.247 This grass garden with the contemporary sculpture sitting at the swimming pool's edge was made for Ms. Barbara Slifka's beach house in Sagaponack on Long Island, New York. The planting was done by her friends, W. Oehme and J. Van Sweden.

p.248 The exquisite nymphaeum and *Palazzo Delle Acque* in the historic park at Villa Visconti Borromeo Litta Lainate, near Milan, which had fallen into serious disrepair and neglect, was bought by the Commune of

Lainate in 1971 and restored. Its pebble mosaics are of a rare charm, and the *giochi d'acqua* a new found delight. Thus one would have to put down the dates of construction from the sixteenth to the twentieth century.

p.253 Palazzo Reale di Caserta near Naples consists of many parts, including a *giardino inglese* (English garden) and it is famous for its 3km-long canal known as the Grand Cascade, and its ravishing sculptures. There are also some lovely garden structures. It certainly deserves a visit and is much less crowded than the better known gardens and parks in Europe.
Tel: +39 823 448084
See also note for p.246.

p.257 *Top:* Lyegrove, Badminton, South Gloucestershire is a beautiful seventeenth-century house in a bucolic setting. Its decorative water basin is at a slightly lower level and surrounded by self-seeding flowers. And guess what: it seems it is for sale!! Google it.
Bottom: The swimming pool was built by the late Dr. Beat Raaflaub in his garden in western Switzerland. Noteworthy are the flowers growing around the pool, in a new Beth Chatto style.

p.260 This garden on Long Island, New York, sadly no longer exists. Russell Page made it for Mr. and Mrs. William Paley, and like much of his work it is well documented.
The Russell Page Archive is housed at the Garden Museum in London.
gardenmuseum.org.uk

Acknowledgements

Above all, I would like to thank Thomas Kramer and Patrick Schneebeli
at Scheidegger & Spiess for their courage and support in publishing this
unorthodox book. The help they gave me is much appreciated.
An equally big Thank You goes to Giulia Biscottini: her inspired design
speaks for itself, and her sensitivity, expertise, and patience made our
collaboration a great pleasure indeed. Thank you also to Nicola Morris
for her corrections and the entertaining phone calls we had. And,
of course, I must not forget my editors of old, namely Leslie Stoker
and Ruth Peltason in New York, who gave me valuable advice at the early
stages of this book project and pointed me in the right direction.
Words hardly suffice to thank Carlo and Stefano Fabro of Carlocolor
in Milan. Their first-rate laboratory work has been of help to me for over
thirty-five years, in both analogue and digital photography.
Only photographers know what a decisive role one's photo lab has.
Heartfelt thanks also to all the garden owners who allowed me to take
photographs of their wonderful places. Without their generosity this
book would look incomplete.
Many thanks for their help with details to Aloisa Moncada and Maria
Stewart Wilson, and to Judith Goldman for her good suggestions.

In a more general way I would like to express my cordial gratitude to my
friends Federico Forquet and Madison Cox, who both have been a source
of inspiration and prompt help whenever it was needed, as well as to
Giuppi Pietromarchi for sharing her exuberance and horticultural passion
with me for so many decades.
And last but not least, my everlasting gratitude goes to my parents, long
dead, for the wonderful upbringing they gave me, and for opening my
eyes to the importance of art as soon as I could walk and talk.

Concept and photography *Marina Schinz*
Design *Giulia Biscottini*
Copy editing, proofreading *Nicola Morris*

Production Director *Sophie Kullmann*
Reprographic work, printing and binding *Verona Libri, Italy*

Despite best efforts, we have not been able to identify all owners of
gardens shown in this book. Individuals or institutions for whom
incorrect or no information is given are asked to contact the
publisher with corrections that can be considered for later editions.

Verlag Scheidegger & Spiess
Niederdorfstrasse 54
8001 Zürich
Switzerland
www.scheidegger-spiess.ch

Scheidegger & Spiess is being supported by the Federal Office
of Culture with a general subsidy for the years 2021–2024.

ISBN 978-3-03942-195-4